MOM, I'M ALL RIGHT

by

KATHLEEN SANDEFER

Edited by

MARY ELIZABETH KRAUEL

Cover Design by LeGrand & Associates

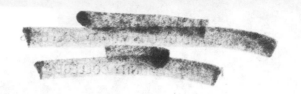

First Printing, 1990
Second Printing, 1990
Third Printing, 1991

Published by: Kathleen Sandefer

For information or permission to use material from the book, contact (in writing) Jackson Enterprises, P.O. Box 493, Coushatta, Louisiana 71019.

Printed in the United States of America
by
Sanders Printing Co.
Garretson, South Dakota

ISBN 0-9626227-0-2

ACKNOWLEDGMENTS

With love and gratitude I wish to name some of the people who have supported me in this effort, although unknowingly:

My dear friends, Liz and Rhonda.

My beautiful Aunt Anne for our long talks about facing the loss of our children.

My wonderful cousins, Toni, Rebecca, Donna, and Susan, for their direction and encouragement.

My Aunt Blanche and Uncle Len for their understanding and concern for me.

My children's beloved Grandmother, Blanche Sandefer.

Posthumous acknowledgment to Mrs. Martha Stephens, who urged me time and again to share my writing after she read my poem, "Christmas Angels." "Mrs. Martha" endured pain and personal loss with grace and unyielding faith in our Lord. She was an inspiration to all who knew her.

To Jan and Wes.

My deepest thanks to Mary Elizabeth Krauel, who patiently arranged so many pieces of remembrances, written narratives, poems, and outpourings of grief into a manuscript, and who said, "First, you must tell the story."

This book is lovingly dedicated to my daughter Shea, who unselfishly allowed me to tell her story here, in part; to Mother and Daddy, from whom I have received love, strength, and faith; to my brother "Tej" and his wife Eileen, who were with me in my darkest hour; and to my sister Rachel, who listened and listened and listened . . .

FOREWORD

The question right after a suicide is not "Why?" but "How can I live with this?" With God's help, I have survived. Whether you believe in God or not, perhaps my testimony will help you work your way through your torment. At least you will be reading words from one who has lived through one of the greatest tragedies a parent can experience. Sometimes you will think you simply cannot bear the suffering.

I hope this book will help you to endure. It will be extremely difficult for you, but I did, you can, and we will go on to live out our lives, accepting the fact that what has happened can never be changed.

I will tell how I coped—sometimes not very well—and am still coping. If my story helps just one person to know that there is someone else who really understands the anguish and pain experienced by the suicide of a child or any loved one, then my efforts will not have been in vain.

"The big star,
Is way out far
On the moonlight
When it's bright
Where will I be,
When I get to see
That big star again?

Weston Sandefer
Age 8
Louisiana

CHAPTER 1

Weston, my second born child, arrived into this world on July 10, 1972. My labor had been induced so that I could return as soon as possible to a teaching position. Wes had not been planned, but we were thrilled at the birth of our son. He was welcomed into the family by a sister, Carolyn Shea, whom we called Shea, then two and one-half years old. She was a bright, loving, and precocious child. Throughout my pregnancy, having already given birth to a girl, I knew the expected baby had to be a boy. Into the eighth month, the baby inside me would somersault heavily and stretch a tiny foot as hard as possible into my side. "Just like a little man," I thought, "to be impervious to the discomfort of a woman, already needing space to grow, to stretch out, to be free!" Yes, I knew it would be a boy.

Rick, my husband, was still in law school at that time, and I was at the lowest pay scale for teachers. We had no insurance to help us with hospital costs. Nevertheless, the birth of a son gave me the feeling of having completed the "perfect" American family—a boy and a girl. Names for this child had been turned over in our minds, but now his father, caught up in the pride and excitement of the event, decided the morning after his birth that he should be called Richard after him. A middle name, Weston, was chosen from the paternal family choices. His name quickly became "Wes" to all of us.

Rick and I grew up in two different family units. He was the only son of a young widowed mother with one other child, a daughter named Sandy, who was one year older than Rick. My family, on the other hand, seemed to be bursting at the seams. There were four of us children, one boy, the eldest, and three girls, all of whom were grown and had children by the time Wes was born. Weston would be the youngest grandchild for several years.

Rick's sister, Sandy, could not have children due to diabetes complications. She was married, living happily in the country, and working as a nurse.

Life in Rick's home was quiet, controlled, serene. Life in my parents' home, with all of us visiting, was chaotic, fun, and, at times, emotionally draining.

We were all adjusting to different "beginnings," while wrestling with our private financial woes, desires, goals, and fears. But for me, order had come into the whirl of changes and the blurred pattern of existence. Rick and I had our family complete. Our lives were laid out before us. Only good things should happen for a long, long time. Rick made Law Review that year, and his career as an attorney loomed realistically ahead.

However, less than a year after Weston was born, Sandy, then only 28 years old, died after surgery to alleviate a condition caused by the diabetes. Overnight, she was gone. I realized happiness was a brittle thing. My mother-in-law would not be the same for a long time, and I had no way of knowing what to do to help her.

Sandy's death was my first experience in womanhood with the sudden loss of a young family member close to me and mine. She was a very important part of our family structure. Shea had been born on her birthday, November 6, and Sandy was my children's only aunt on that side of the family. She was only one year older than I but seemed much wiser. From her I learned the calming benefits of reading. We had long talks while floating lazily in the swimming pool or sitting up late at night. Although she was tiny in stature, she had more courage than anyone I knew at that time in my life. I experienced the natural phenomenon of wanting to get all the pieces back together again but was confronted with the helplessness death presents.

Rick had dealt with a lot during his lifetime. He had lost his father when he was only sixteen, lost his best friend in a tragic drowning accident before we married, lived through being injured in Viet Nam, and seen many close friends die in the war. He steeled himself to the loss of his sister, but I was totally distraught. I wanted to bring her back, to deny that things would never be the same for our family again. He did not relate to my grief, and we did not talk.

I had been determined to give my son all the right beginnings. I attempted breastfeeding but gave it up after three months. By then, I had already returned to school teaching full time for almost eight weeks. Mental torture from leaving my small baby had begun to plague me even before the actual time came to go back to work. Luckily, we found a young woman who was willing to accept the low wages I could pay for being a nursemaid to Wes and sitter for Shea. At least they could be kept at home instead of being carted off to a less acceptable nursery arrangement. Allean, our new babysitter, was sincerely fond of both children, and they loved her. For the time being, things seemed to be on an even keel. Rick would finish law school in another year, and we planned to buy an older, but larger, home for our growing family. The future looked brighter.

The months between infancy and toddlerhood passed normally as expected for Wes. The only remarkable difference in this stage of development was that he had to have casts on both legs and feet to correct a near-club foot condition diagnosed by his pediatrician. Wes would not sleep through the night. It seemed cruel for such a small child to have to tolerate heavy binding casts with a steel bar between them. He accepted it almost passively, so when he developed a rocking habit soon after he learned to sit up, I didn't think it strange, considering he had very little freedom of movement. His crying at night and restless sleep were attributed to discomfort.

I did not consult the pediatrician until after the removal of the casts and stationary bar when the crying and frequent awakening still continued with increased intensity. Wes was nearly two then, but the doctor did not make the slightest comment or suggestion other than to dose the baby with a little red medicine in his nighttime bottle. The medicine did not help at all. In fact, the medicine that was supposed to make him sleep seemed to have an opposite reaction. It made him scream until he was hoarse, and he would pull and shake his baby bed while I either ran back and forth to the kitchen for bottles or stood helplessly by trying to soothe him. I would rock him far into the night until my head was dropping from exhaustion and he would finally give up for four blissful hours.

CHAPTER 2

Wes learned to crawl out of his baby bed, climb down, and find his way to a couch in the den. There on the couch, in the wee hours of the morning, he would rock himself. He cried for attention less frequently now, except for the bottle which he would hold as he rocked. I can still see him, sitting erect with his eyes closed, rocking back and forth and then leaning to the side as he would drop off to sleep, only to awaken and renew his rocking as if driven by some unseen force. Most nights I would go into the den and watch him. He would, by choice, want the couch to himself. He didn't want me to touch him or interfere with his rocking mission. I don't know when or why we accepted it as "his way." Our nights were disrupted, but no one knew what to do. It was just a part of our lives each night to see Weston slamming himself hard against the couch and watch him doze, wake up, and start the rocking all over again until he fell into an exhausted sleep. Then we could finally put him back into his bed. I became accustomed to listening for him, losing much needed sleep, and coping with a back condition from continuously lifting him and getting in and out of bed.

Even though Weston resisted being held and rocked, he was loving and sweet. The oddities were, perhaps, made less monumental to us because he was so beautiful and normal to look at. Unlike most small children, he had no fear of being alone while he rocked in a darkened room. He liked to have his father hold him and would fall asleep in his strong arms. But soon after Rick put him down in the bed and went back to sleep, Wes was awake again, and it was back to the nightly pattern.

Although he wouldn't talk, Wes was developing an inter-

esting personality. Rick and I thought it was particularly hi-
larious that one of Weston's favorite ways of expressing himself
was to have you hold him stretched out while supporting his
head and bottom as one would hold an infant. He would act like
a helpless, mewling baby. He would do this for as long as you
could hold him, and by now he was pretty heavy. I remember
laughing but thinking how his facial expressions and infantile
grunting made him seem retarded. It did make me uneasy. He
was an odd little boy, but he was my baby.

At two, he was walking and running in corrective shoes,
an active physically healthy child, but was not talking except
in single words. He would go to the door and say "souside" for
outside or simply "cookie" for a snack. A rare sentence would
be, "I want botter," for his bottle. I compensated and allowed
him to keep his bottle not only because he had never liked a
pacifier but also probably as much for my hopes to keep him
asleep at night and not to aggravate his already severe restlessness. When Wes could open the refrigerator door, I put the bottles where he could just reach inside and get one for himself.

By this time, I was totally stressed out from the nightly
lack of sleep, financial problems, the almost non-communicative
relationship with my husband, and the demands of my teaching job. It was all I could do to hold everything together, including the housework, aggravations with an older house, disabling
backaches, two pre-school children, and a deteriorating marriage. Rick had his own goals and professional dreams which
contributed to his shunning of domestic responsibilities. He was
soon to receive his law degree. I saw less and less of him and
resented him more and more. At this period in our lives, all I
knew was work, work, and more work; worry, worry, and more
worry. While he deliberately stayed out of my way, I felt
neglected. I needed rest. I needed and wanted support as well
as reassurance that I hadn't been just a ticket to his commence-
ment day.

I wanted things some way, somehow, to get better. Where
once Rick and I enjoyed playing our guitars together, singing to
and cuddling our two children in bed on Saturday mornings,

we became desensitized to our relationship. We acted like strangers to one another.

I reverted to a destructive adolescent habit I had developed at fourteen when dealing with stressful times. I began to pull out my hair, strand by strand, more and more. This shackled me with another worry: how to hide bald spots on my head at work. I felt so unattractive. I knew I looked worse than I had ever looked in my life, but I could not have cared less. I gained weight, had no time for personal interests; demands for conversation from my husband ended in snatchy terse remarks. My marriage was crumbling at the edges with a big black hole in the middle into which I was falling. I was angry and defensive. I reserved all of my patience for the students at school and Weston.

Shea entered kindergarten about this time. She was only a few months past the age of four, but I felt she was ready after those years spent at home with her small brother and a maid. Shea was bright and gregarious. Her father provided much of her emotional support, and they were very close, for which I was thankful. However, I felt that Weston did not receive his fair share of attention from his father. So, I was my son's mentor and sole caretaker, with no small feeling of resentment.

When Shea's kindergarten teacher called in the very beginning hours of school to say that Shea was screaming in a corner of the room and refusing to mind her, I was shocked. Shea was not a docile child at home but was usually cooperative and manageable. More than anything, she displayed maturity and courage beyond her years. Perhaps having been left to her own devices while I paid so much attention to Wes, she felt her premature independence being threatened for the first time. This didn't last long, however. Soon she fell into the normal acceptable behavior for a pre-schooler and learned quickly. No other problems were ever reported except that she did not like nap time. Her grades were excellent.

At home, Shea was sweet and kind to her little brother. Many times she would interpret his wishes for him since Wes still

refused to talk very much in whole sentences. He didn't care
to be read to by anyone but her. She did not mind his rocking
next to her while she read. Sometimes, I would see them rock
together, both seeming to relish the feeling of the rhythmical
motion. I remember thinking that maybe this was just something that my children liked to do, but Shea stopped. Wes
continued on and on, endlessly, several times a day.

When our beloved babysitter had to quit working because
her own baby was soon due, Wes continued rocking as though
in a catatonic state while we went through a series of poor
replacements. Finally, with other problems compounding the
homebound situation, I searched for another childcare solution.
His grandmother, my mother-in-law, commented one day that
she had stopped by to look in on him and was very concerned
about his seeming disinterest in anything and his not being
stimulated by the latest new maid. She then volunteered to
keep Wes in her home.

Everyone involved with Weston's development when he
was three was dumbfounded with his frustrating refusal to
make any headway in toilet training, which would be the big-
gest step toward making the care of him easier and making
life a little more bearable for us all. Wes got the urinating in the
potty down pretty well, but he steadfastly refused to give up
the bowel movement in his diapers. I was so determined to help
him along that I kept him in training pants all day and diaper-
ed him at night. We all tried. We tried rewards, long quiet times
in the bathroom, and even mild reprimands—to no avail. It was
becoming obvious now that he lived in a little world all his
own.

CHAPTER 3

My marriage began to fail rapidly. Rick and I fought episodic bouts. Each new argument included old ones, and nothing was ever forgiven or resolved. I felt like I was caught in a vise that just had to be tolerated, for the alternative (losing him) was worse. By now, the responsibility of Wes had become too much of a burden for his grandmother. Shea was becoming irritable and rebellious when punished. I was constantly tensed up and ready for the blows as they came. And they did come—financial problems, school problems, physical problems, along with marital problems.

When Rick finally left, we had gone through periods of intense anger with each other. Shea was disturbed by the events. The only one who seemed oblivious to the circumstances was Wes.

After the separation, I tried very hard to get my life organized. Organization is a defense mechanism I use in times of crisis. The more disheveled my emotional and spiritual life become, the more organization I must have. Weston's toilet training kept things in an upheaval. Nursery schools refused to take toddlers over three and a half years old who were still not toilet trained. In my frustration, I even forced children's enemas on Wes on two occasions to try to make him understand what he was supposed to do on the commode. He only cried in fear and bewilderment and then, after I had given up waiting for results, went off both times and had the bowel movements in his pants. When he turned four years old, my determination to succeed to potty train him became an obsession. I felt ashamed for us both that I could not do what I needed to do to help him, thus creating a constant worry and feeling of failure. Wes seemed unmoved by it all.

The summer after his fourth birthday I asked his pediatrician about it, and he recommended a child psychologist. I had no money and still no solution for Weston's daycare. The new school year was about to begin. Alone and responsible for the care of my two children, I thought of nothing but getting both children settled so I could work.

Finally, and fortunately, I called a highly recommended day school which was located right in our neighborhood but was quite expensive for my budget. I listened with elation as the schoolmaster asked me to give them a chance to toilet train Weston before taking him to a psychologist. Any amount of tuition was worth this to me. They completed the job within just three months. I counted the other advantages against the additional strain on my finances: He would be exposed to pre-kindergarten skills and could interact with other children his own age; it would be a head start for him; he would, perhaps, come out of his close little imaginary world and reach for normalcy. I did not admit the last point to myself in those terms, but I am very sure that, subconsciously, the hope was there.

I had been optimistic that the private school would accelerate Weston's development, but realistically, other than for the toilet training, I saw little or no progress. Their program was designed for the advancement of kindergartners, but at the age of five when Wes entered public school kindergarten, I knew he hadn't achieved any higher level, and his marks even showed him to be behind.

At the end of the year, the teacher recommended that Wes be held back. His behavioral marks were dominated with L's for "Limited Progress" and N's for "Needs Improvement." Weston had started talking because of the intensive training at the private school, and now he talked incessantly, much of the time only to himself.

Wes looked at books and made up the stories to go with the pictures. His writing and drawing were very immature compared to the other children's. From that early age and throughout most of his school years, incomplete work and inattention were the chief complaints of his teachers.

There we were—Shea, at seven, clashing with me and missing her father but behaving beautifully in school; Wes, with more problems than any little fellow should have before embarking on a long school career; and me, an emotionally drained, insecure, lonely young divorcee, mother, and teacher.

During the next two years, I recklessly sought companionship and tried to create a totally new social life for myself. I took up tennis and made new friends. I dated indiscriminately. I was dutifully attentive to the children's basic needs, but for the most part neglectful. How I crammed everything in, I'll never know. It was as if all those years of hardly sleeping had adapted me for a night life of going, going, going, at home or out, while still functioning as an elementary school teacher.

After the divorce, I found new organization. I kept the yard, redecorated my house, budgeted my money, bought new clothes, and lost lots of weight. I looked and felt as good as I ever had felt except for the bouts of loneliness and depression.

My greatest support during this time was my sister Jan, two years younger than I, who also lived in Baton Rouge. We spoke on the telephone every day, and she listened patiently to my tearful stories, my angry reactions to injustices I believed myself and children to be suffering, my need for love, acceptance, and understanding. She was my best friend. She could make me laugh when everything else around me seemed shattered. Jan had two sons; her son, Will, and Shea were only six months apart in age and very close, almost like brother and sister. Her other son, Brown, was three years younger than Wes. We were together countless times, playing with our children, observing and discussing them. Jan shared all my concerns about Weston's problems. I don't know what my life in those years would have been like without her.

During peaceful moments at home, I would sit alone in the den and play the guitar or watch TV. I began to settle in emotionally and found new strength spiritually. I even began to write music and words for songs. Eventually, I made a record with one of the songs that described how I felt about my life with Rick. All of this, of course, stemmed from my need to re-build my confidence and reconcile myself to a failed marriage—the loss of my dream of the happy family. I demanded every-thing from myself and forgave myself for nothing.

Rick was gone from our lives for long intervals. I mourned, cried anew, and fought off long periods of depression after each of his infrequent visits to the children. One night in my ex-plosive state, Wes did something that angered me. I grabbed for him. To escape from me, he ran straight into the oven door and hit it hard with his face. As I cradled him in remorse when I saw his bloodied little nose, Shea came up to me and said, "Mama, you are scaring me." I looked at my children and decided then and there that they would not be victims. I had to get hold of myself for all of our sakes and let go of this indulgence in my own emotions.

I eventually took pride in my determination to go it alone. "Do it without help" was my motto. We adjusted, and the three of us became quite a crew. Shea led Wes to school in the mornings and home in the afternoons. She helped him remember his books and coat. They walked less than a block to the elementary school in our neighborhood. I counted each and every element such as this one a blessing. A lineup of babysitters came and went for after-school watch until I could get home. I never left the children alone. Shea became very dependable and seemed aware of her little brother's special needs.

I don't know exactly when I realized Wes was accident prone, nor do I know if I thought it was abnormal. I do know that my subconscious mind began to dwell on my son's safety after many inexplicable incidents that were hazardous to him. For example, he fell into his grandmother's pool during the winter with the rain-filled cover still on top, and he ran across the hot floor furnace, fell, and burned both hands and feet. Even in the same house with him, I couldn't relax. I constantly checked on him at intervals I deemed necessary. Once he wandered off in the neighborhood, hid in a tool shed until dark, and I had to call the police. I feared each and every day of his youth that he would forget to look both ways and step out in front of a car, walk in front of the school bus and not move out of its path fast enough, electrocute himself with just about anything electrical, cut himself with sharp objects, dive into shallow water, fall from heights, etc. Each year I hoped the feeling of being braced for disaster might pass. It just wasn't natural for a mother to live with such fears, but I lived with them just the same. The feeling of apprehension about the possibility of danger to Wes never went away until his death.

CHAPTER 4

My neighbor, Julie, was at least six years younger than I, but she was one of those women who seemed to have it all pulled together. After we met for the first time, we laughed about all the coincidental things we had in common. She had been a Phi Mu in college, finished in elementary education, her maiden name was Jackson, and she married a man named Sandifer. I had been a Phi Mu, finished in education, my maiden name was Jackson, and I married a man named Sandefer. Now we lived next door to each other and became quite close. Another thing we shared in common was that we were both Baptists. Only that was where I found the greatest difference between us. Julie was a good Baptist. I was a backslider. Whenever I was around her, I felt her goodness and spirit. I knew she never had an evil thought, or if she did, she would be filled with remorse and be instantly forgiven by God. She was truly one of His sheep if I ever knew one.

Julie knew about my marital problems. I was confused and bitter, even angry with the Lord about the whole mess I found myself in. One Saturday morning, Julie knew Rick had taken the children with him for the weekend. I was set to enjoy a few hours of unencumbered peace when she came over and asked me to join her on an excursion downtown that afternoon to attend a young women's seminar. She was determined to get me to go, and I made her promise it was not going to be some religious program that would turn out to be endless and boring. On the way, I remember feeling trapped in her car and in a no-turn-back situation. My feelings seemed confirmed when we arrived, and I saw at least a hundred young women milling around with Bibles in their hands.

The speakers began to go up to the podium before all the women gathered in the long rows of seats. (I had lost Julie by this time.) People got very quiet, and one by one different women spoke. I became totally engrossed when one woman told a story that paralleled my own, but she had found grace to live and live well. Other stories moved me even more. My feelings of being lost and alone, deserted and hurt, began to fall away. I knew now that I was there for a purpose. Julie had tricked me. I was sure that she had been the Lord's instrument. Later, at lunch, I still had not located Julie. I sat with a group of women, none of whom I knew, but I immediately felt comfortable with them. A beautiful girl, sitting on my right, began to talk to me and soon had me pouring out my sorrowful story. She began to gently minister to me, and I never had experienced such direct spiritual communication with a complete stranger. I was further convinced that I was there because of the Lord's will and that the results would be a change in my life forever.

After lunch, the girl, Rainey, and I moved out into the hotel lobby where we found a quiet corner so we could talk. She asked me if I felt that I was saved, and I told her, frankly, that I did not. Hearing my own words surprised me. The honesty of admitting that I had been a Christian since the age of eight but at thirty did not feel as if I were saved was a revelation to me. We prayed, and I felt washed clean, forgiven. On the way home I prayed that this feeling of complete happiness and freedom from worry along with the grace of God would never leave me. I would make a change in my lifestyle due to this experience, but the complete acknowledgment of God as Master of my life was not to last.

At home, I resolved to make the changes in my life that were needed and prayed, with God's help, I might find some solutions to problems that plagued me. These problems included inadequate care of my children, more attention for Weston than the public school was providing, an unhappy relationship with the wrong man, and, of course, the feeling of not "belonging" anymore. My best single friend was getting married. I had tired of the disgusting "fishing expeditions" in the single bars at night.

I knew that I needed to get away from many things and go toward something—a good healthy change for us all.

One afternoon I was turning these thoughts over and over in my mind. Finally, I went to the bookshelf and took my Bible down. I simply said to the Lord, "If you want me to do something about my life, please direct me and guide me to what it should be." I opened the Bible and quickly read a single verse: "I will return to the nest to die." I looked up. My eyes scanned the rooms I could see in the house. These rooms had meant home to me for the past six years. Leave all this? Leave Jan? I'll do it. I'll go home. Jan and I can be together when she comes home for visits. God wants me to go home, and I can trust God now. The turn of events that followed bordered on the miraculous.

The house we lived in was an old, unattractive red brick structure with an ugly carport, which had been built on later. The yard was shaped like a wedge of pie with so many unkempt large oaks that grass would only grow in patches. The roof had filled with water that began to cause leaks. Once I opened the door, which led out onto the carport, and a current of water fell into the room just like an ocean wave. I was constantly fighting roaches, and the leaves from the oaks fell relentlessly, threatening to bury what little grass there was.

Rick had completed some amateur carpentry projects before we separated. These projects combined with some other unique improvements we did together were features that a realtor might use to sell the old house. And after the divorce, I bought something I had always wanted, a piano. I had little extra money, but I found a piano which looked as much like my grandmother's as possible, an old King upright. Once I proudly beheld it sitting there against the living room wall, I rationalized that Shea could learn to play the piano.

Now, I was contemplating leaving all this. By this time Rick had moved away, and my last hopes for a reconciliation were gone. I would leave, too. Bittersweet memories were in the walls of this home that had seen divorce.

A few days later I was introduced in church to a young woman who had recently begun a real estate agency. I spoke with her about selling my house, and she listened to my story about finding the Lord's will in my Bible. We both became very excited about the possibility of getting me moved back to my hometown—back where I was supposed to be. I began to visualize it in my mind. I would be back with my parents; no more teaching in an impossible situation; the children would be surrounded by family; I would have my old friends and a new job; I would belong to the church of my youth and possibly even teach Sunday School; we would belong to the Country Club and go to the lake as much as we wanted to. Oh, how I looked forward to it! A slower, rural country life would be my salvation. There was no doubt in my mind. The only obstacle was to sell the old house with broken-down plumbing and a bad roof. My realtor was confident.

The very next week, an ad for the house was listed in the paper. My house sounded like the buy of the century. The only couple that came to look at the house loved the neighborhood, the quiet street, the old-fashioned architecture of the other houses on the street, the azaleas and the bay window, but they didn't seem to like the house itself much. The deal was struck when the husband turned at the front door as they were leaving and asked, "Will the piano stay?"

I thought he was joking, and I replied, "If you'll buy the house, it will."

"Okay," he said, and they left.

In a few days, the realtor called to say that the buyers had countered her list price only once. Would I accept? Would I? We had bought the old home for much less than I was asking. I felt like I had stumbled onto a gold mine. "The piano will have to stay as well as the curtains," she said and hung up. I had paid $400.00 for the piano and had made the curtains myself.

The sale of the house was closed within 30 days. The Lord moved pretty fast, in my opinion. There was no turning back now. I began to make preparations to resign my job and find a mover.

CHAPTER 5

During the month before we moved, I found my way back
to the Lord and found, too, an inner strength and peace I never
thought possible. I was not a born-again Christian. My experience was more that of a lost Christian being accepted back into
the fold.

I would listen to my children's prayers at night. The
innocence of little children concerning things of the spirit is a
wonder and joy to behold. It brings to mind the verse in which
Jesus tells the doubting adults to leave the little children alone
because the kingdom of God belongs to them. Shea would, at
the end of her prayer (just as I had done when a child) bless cats
and dogs and other animals. Wes would repeat the words of
the prayer slowly with such sweet "curling" of the words that I
knew he had no idea what they meant. One night, I sat on the
edge of his bed and listened to his repeating each line after me
when, suddenly, after saying a part out loud, "I pray the Lord,
my soul to keep," he cried out, "Mama, I want my soul to keep!"
I just laughed at his innocent interpretation of the prayer,
whatever it was, and kissed him goodnight.

Loss of innocence befell my son at an early age. With all
the miracles that were occurring, things were not going as
smoothly as I believed. One afternoon I returned home to let
the babysitter go and soon started out the door with both children
for a trip to the grocery store. Shea tugged on my arm and stopped me at the top of the steps. "Mama," she said.

Wes began to scream, "Don't tell! Don't tell!" He was so
violently upset that he turned red. Outbursts like this from
Wes were unnatural. I quickly calmed him down by telling Shea
not to say anything to me that Wes didn't want her to.

The urgency in Shea's voice assured me that she would tell me when we were alone together. Later that evening when Wes had gone to sleep, we sat together, and my eight year old daughter told me that one of the babysitters had made Wes take off all his clothes. Then she took off hers and made him lie on top of her. He confessed this to Shea when she came back from a neighbor's house where she had been playing with a school friend.

Wes only knew enough about sex to know that little boys had genitals different from little girls, but he knew what had happened had been shameful and upsetting. We never spoke about it again. I called the babysitter and told her what had been revealed to me and that I thought she was sick and needed help. Whether the accusations were true or not, I just knew that I needed to remove the threat of harm to Wes.

I will never know how much, or if, the experience made an impression on his young mind that he carried with him beyond his six years. I do know that at this point, he had two new fears: fear of the water and fear of someone seeing his naked body.

This incident confirmed my decision to move as soon as possible. Now I was even more determined to leave this house of sad memories that had lost all its appeal for me. Fervently believing that God was still working in my life, I set my course on the task of moving home.

Ironically, when I left my small hometown for college, I vowed I would never return again to live there. However, now I needed to return to my "nest" and be near my family. I would end this part of my life and start anew. I would forget the stress and anguish of an unhappy marriage. But I did not know at all what lay ahead.

When I reached impulsively for my Bible over a month earlier, I had said, "Lord, if you will tell me what to do, I will obey your instructions. I need your help." And obey I did. I packed my belongings, the children, two parakeets, and a cat named Lucifer, and moved home.

CHAPTER 6

I will always remember the freedom I felt when we pulled away from the old house. All the way back home, the children and I sang. It was summer, but we sang, "Over the river and
through the woods/To Grandmother's house we go!" We sang it
again and again, laughing together. My feelings were infect-
ious, and I was glad. I wanted them to be happy about the move,
and more than anything, I wanted them to be healed from the
hurt I knew they both suffered from the divorce and long
separations from their father.

We settled into our little rented house in July 1979. I
turned my attention to getting the children enrolled in school. I
decided on a small private school about fifteen miles away. They
had to ride the school bus which was quite different from the
very short walk each morning to their old school. At first they
liked the change, but it wasn't long before getting up very early
in the morning and the long ride to school became drudgery.

We had a nice little two bedroom frame house near the
highway which was easy to keep clean. The bonus was a big red
barn behind it complete with a pasture where we could keep a
pony if we desired. There was also a circular drive on which
the children could play. Wes, then seven, had still not learned
to ride a bicycle. Shea's goal was to teach him before he would
be embarrassed by someone his own age or of the age to which
it would matter. She worked all day, running beside the tiny
bicycle on the driveway. Time and time again Wes would let the
bike lean to the side, but Shea would hold him upright. Although
she was only a little bigger than he, she held up the bicycle
and encouraged him to pedal faster. Her efforts finally paid off.
She was as proud of him as he was of himself. The two child-

ren were bonded and always loving toward each other. Wes trusted her, and her patience exceeded most adults'. They frequently planned their games together and played until nightfall; they seldom fought.

Before school started, Shea quickly got into the swing of small town summer life. She met and made new friends, enjoyed the local library, took swimming and diving lessons. Wes still was somewhat afraid of the water and preferred the shallow pool. The club manager complained that Wes was too large and rambunctious for the tiny babies who did not like water in their faces; so, many times Weston was shooed out. Finally, with the prodding of his big sister, he would go down into the big pool with the other children and play along the side, but as soon as the opportunity allowed, he was back in the baby pool. He also preferred the company of the toddlers and the younger children. He was sweet and gentle with them, talking to little boys and girls alike in such an engaging way that most of the time watchful parents did not mind his presence in the small pool.

We took our annual fourth of July vacation at the lake, and Wes fell in love with fishing. He would stand on the bank for hours with line and pole waiting for a fish to nibble. He did not mind being alone while he fished. Several times he caught one and came running up to the cabin to proudly and excitedly display his catch. He never tired of this kind of pastime. He loved fishing so much that several times we drove over to the lake on an afternoon, and I would sit on the grass and watch him.

Late that summer, it was time for me to start the training for my new job as a representative for an insurance company in Oklahoma. My brother and his family lived in Tulsa, where he was an officer in the company for which I was going to work. I thought it might be a good opportunity for us to visit with them before school started, so we all three set off for Tulsa. The summer was ending, but we could still go to the lake for some skiing and fun between my training sessions.

All of the children (my two and my brother's) were excited the day we went to the lake and launched the boat. My brother's two boys, both good skiers, were impatiently helping their

father get the boat into the water. Weston refused to get into
the boat. At first, I thought a little coaxing from his bigger cousins and Shea would have him cooperating in just a few minutes,
but it only made things worse. Fear was evident in his face,
and now he was crying hard. Finally, in exasperation, his uncle
picked him up and bodily set him inside. He huddled down on
the floor of the boat, and I felt so sorry for him that I offered to
stay on land so that they could go out peacefully. My brother
shook off my suggestion, and we drove out onto the lake.

I wanted to hold Wes and comfort him. I also wanted to go
home. He finally stopped crying but sat miserably in the hot
boat while each of the other children skied and swam.

I was never able to predict the actions of my own child.
With all the help and encouragement he received from everyone, he was still a fearful, unsure little boy, lacking coordination
or even confidence in any endeavor. The summer before we left
Baton Rouge, we had tried Tee Ball in the park with the small
children's ball teams. Wes, six years old, would only stand out
in the field, sometimes with his back to the playing field, or sit
down on the ground and play in the dirt, paying no attention to
the game whatsoever. Wes learned no skills and was absolutely
uninterested in competition. His actions were disconcerting to
the other children, but he didn't seem aware of that, either.

He was more content to play alone with small objects such
as rocks, nails, or toy cars. He would sit for hours on a swing
and talk to himself or dig in a sandbox until dark.

Now, here on a vacation in Oklahoma, far away from the
neighborhood from which we had moved, I looked at my child
and wished that I could understand him, help him in some way,
or at least get some indication that he was going to change.

We planned to go see the play *Oklahoma*. Sitting for any
length of time where children needed to be still and quiet was
an impossibility for Wes. His attention span was so short that
an activity of this nature was a trial for everyone involved,
except for church, where he was usually well-behaved. During
the most exciting part of a ballgame, he might be observing
something on the floor or ground. He never understood why

we were there. I saw other children his age absorbed in the outdoor drama, but not Wes.

When we were getting ready for the return trip home from our Oklahoma visit, I was dismayed to hear my sister-in-law remark about how many times she had washed the sheets Wes slept on. I was in such a habit of stripping the bed once, and sometimes twice, during the night that I had really forgotten how inconvenient it must have been for her. Wes still wet the bed nightly at home, and I guess I just adapted to it as I had to the waking and crying for four years previously. I apologized sincerely and told her I had done everything I knew to help him stop.

I was acutely aware of the damage to Weston's self esteem by his failure to control bedwetting at seven years of age. I avoided out of home overnight stays. Camps and spending the night with other children were out of the question until he was ten when we discovered that a medication could have helped him all along. I constantly protected Wes from humiliation. It was obvious he could not help the bedwetting, so I did not chastise him for it. It had become a minor problem to me. At least he was sleeping, and so was I. To just get up once at night and check him, move him to change his sheets, put them in the washer, and get back into bed was wonderful. After a while the major problem was the smell of the urine, and plastic sheets and mattresses had to be discarded. I never spoke to him about it except to give encouragement. Limiting fluid intake and reminding him to go to the bathroom before bedtime were the only things I knew to do. Sometimes it worked. I praised him when he went all night without wetting the bed, but these few and far between times did not signal a big change.

Another habit he had that persisted and became a nuisance was his rocking back and forth. I had to insist he stop doing it in the car. It seemed to rock the whole car as we drove along because he pounded so hard. The motion soothed him and kept him pacified, so I usually relented on long trips. His rocking annoyed Shea, too, but he rocked and rocked all the way home from Tulsa.

CHAPTER 7

Back at home, the opening of school presented new problems and adjustments. I had high hopes for Weston's progress because the teachers were mostly friends with whom I had gone to school. I knew they were caring and dedicated teachers, and I hoped Wes would get special attention and understanding. I ignored the suggestion from his teacher the year before that he be held back, continuing to deny the real signs of his broken development. I attributed his lack of motivation and immaturity to separation from his father and our divorce, and I couldn't bring myself to let him experience another setback.

The teachers at this new private school lived up to all my expectations. Wes made good grades, and no outstanding problems were reported. His handwriting skills lacked control, but he learned reading, spelling, and English skills readily. He also absorbed math at a normal rate. I was not aware of the intensive efforts the teachers were making with him nor the limits of patience he tested. I only knew that the teachers were kind and related to me that they enjoyed teaching him. Their main complaints were that he needed to pay closer attention in class and complete his assignments on time. I had been a teacher myself for over nine years and knew that different children had special needs and would settle down when handled properly.

Wes was usually malleable and seldom needed harsh discipline. He wanted to please, but he was so easily distracted. He was especially difficult on certain days. I knew when he had to constantly be reminded to do little tasks at home, when he lost track of time and became absorbed in something other than what he was supposed to be doing, that the same behavior had to be evident in school. But, I thought, "He's young and will grow out of it, surely."

Growth, however, has many diverse facets in children. Physical growth is easily observable. Maturation of the emotions, socialization, and educational growth is subtle. Wes was growing at a normal rate physically, but his emotional and social maturity were lagging far behind. Other children would look at him in funny ways or comment on his strange expressions or incessant talking. Sometimes they just tuned him out. I observed this and felt miserable for him. Wes continued to play with much younger children with whom he was more compatible and who tolerated him best. Because they were less given to cruelty and did not taunt him, I was content, also.

One of the best parts about life in the country out on his grandparents' place was the woods, or the "forests" as Wes called them. He could spend lots of time walking and looking for rabbits, squirrels, deer, and bird nests. He would pretend and imagine all sorts of things. He was always inclined to imaginings that became real to him. He would come back with various stories about what he had seen in the forest: tracks, feathers, snakes, etc. Sometimes, he even brought them along with him to prove stories.

That first winter back home it snowed. The children delighted in playing outside in it. This event began Wes' love affair with the snow. Every winter just the threat of snow excited him.

For Christmas, I bought Shea a pony and saddle. I wanted to do something special for her. She shared a love of horses with me and her Aunt Sandy. The pony arrived with two red bows— one on each ear. Shea was thrilled! She took one look and ran across the porch, jumped on its back, and rode around the house four or five times.

We turned the horse out into the pasture, and cousins and friends took turns riding. They all argued over who would get to ride next. Small cousins rode while the pony was led by an adult, and bigger cousins doubled up. Not Wes. He watched briefly and then went back to his new Lincoln Logs, a gift that proved to be a gem for him because he was very creative with them, surprisingly. He patiently built elaborate structures.

New Year's Eve, 1980, we invited boy cousins his age over to shoot fireworks. I supervised the lighting of each candle or firecracker, no matter how independent each child felt he was. There was no competition. Wes loved this, and I loved pleasing him. A new year began.

My traveling as a sales and service representative placed a strain on me when I realized how much I would have to be away from my children, but it also gave me, for the first time in years, an opportunity to see that I could actually do something else with my life. My parents and younger sister, Rachel, rallied to my support. They took over the responsibilities when I was away. The children cooperated most of the time although they had become accustomed to our close life together at home. Picking them up and moving them over to my sister's home or my parents' home became a way of life.

Advantages were there, however. My father and brother-in-law took an interest in Wes, taking him fishing, teaching and encouraging him to do "man's work" around the house. They talked to him and acted as surrogate fathers, something Wes had been deprived of most of his life. We were a good distance away from their father, and visits became more and more infrequent. When the children did see him, it was a shared visit and seldom a one-on-one time for Wes and his father. The two never seemed to bond, and many times I wondered if Rick noted the peculiarities in his son and just could not accept him for who he was. If Weston ever harbored resentment or felt he lacked something in his life, he never expressed it.

When Rick and I spoke, we would argue about money— child support. I became more determined than ever to maintain financial independence, hoping one day I would not need anyone else. This new job was my chance to accomplish it.

We had lived in the little rent house for one year, and it was time to use the proceeds from the sale of our old house to buy a house in our new location. Wes was eight when we moved into the new house in a subdivision with lots of children to play

with.   His room, the first that was not a converted or pass-
through bedroom, was at the end of the hall.   He really liked his
new privacy and having his own domain in a house with two
females. He posted signs on the outside of his door announcing
ownership and hung a sign on the doorknob that read, "Keep
Out! Disaster Area."

CHAPTER 8

During the summer of 1981, I thought it would be a good idea to try Wes again at Tee Ball. The boys who would be playing were friends he had been with in school, and I hoped peer influence would encourage him to put forth more effort. I would get home from work, still dressed in business suit and high heels, and go with him to ball practice. Each time, I pretended to be relaxed in my lawn chair, but I was tense and hoping for a good day on the ball field for Wes. Time and time again he would swing at the ball on the tee and miss completely or hit the tee. When his team went out onto the field, he was assigned to a position where he could do the least damage.

Sometimes, when he had his turn at bat, he would pop the ball lazily toward the pitcher. Before the pitcher could reach it, Wes would luckily make it to first base. I prayed for him to do well and hurt deeply for him when he didn't. I am sure most mothers have the same feelings. But I watched the fathers with their sons and burned with jealousy that this boy, so greatly in need of what I could not give, had to be without.

Shea and I practiced with him. He didn't give up. When he did hit a ball and made it to first base (on rare occasions), the joy was written all over his face. His expression seemed to say, "I've redeemed myself! I'm not great, but sometimes I can be good."

I fretted and worried so much about the situation that I finally shared it with a co-worker, expecting him to sympathize completely. Instead, he told me, with some conviction, that I should stop kicking myself and moaning over the fact that Weston didn't have a father at home to play ball with and just be glad that he was healthy enough to run and throw a ball.

The ball season ended. We collected his little trophy, took

pictures at the coach's party, and went home. Wes fell asleep that night in his league shirt on the floor in the living room, contented in his exhaustion that he saw it through.

I never urged Wes to play ball again, and we never spoke of it at home. He accepted with good grace the gloves, balls, bats, and football equipment given to him over the ensuing years. One last try in the sixth grade to play junior high football with his classmates ended in the same defeat and subsequent humiliation. He told me not to waste my time going to buy an expensive helmet because he wasn't going to play another game after the one we did go to. He "hung it up," so to speak, and I truly was relieved.

Weston's coordination sometimes seemed to come and go. I had his eyes tested, and there was no problem. I decided he might not be able to play ball with the best of them, but he could play and enjoy sports in the neighborhood. I could do very little except to let Wes know that I accepted him the way he was and privately hoped the failed athletic experiences wouldn't hurt too deeply or too long.

When I visited Weston's teachers, I received mixed reviews. They offered comments after discussing his problems like, "Oh, there's nothing wrong with Weston. He's just all boy," or "Sometimes it's hard to get Wes to do his work. I have to sit on him," and always, "But he can do it if he wants to!" How many times did Wes hear that in his lifetime? I wonder if he ever wanted to scream back at all of them, "I want to!" He was literally being beaten down by well-meaning people. I could only stand by helplessly and watch and hope that he could deal with it.

From seven to nine years of age, it became more apparent that Wes was different. He didn't seem to mind it or probably didn't recognize it at this age. My parents and other family members found it amusing the way Weston expressed himself at times. Very often we quoted him as an inside family joke. For example, he would say, "This should fill me down" instead of "up" when taking a second helping of food; "The car is being covered with dark" instead of "shade"; or, "The sun is cracking over the trees." His terminology endeared him to me even more. The hurtful times came when other children began to notice and laugh or to remark about his quirky personality. Wes ignored them, for the most part, and continued to seek the company of younger, kinder children.

I think this way of expressing himself was what his teachers began to observe. At ten, the marked advancement of his peers in emotional maturity made Wes' own immaturity and slow progress more prominent. To make matters worse, Wes began to blink and exhibit eye and facial tics. He also made guttural voice sounds like a repetitive clearing of the throat that irritated those around him. He seemed unaware of both.

The most noticeable sign of immaturity at ten was the total inability to take responsibility for anything. Wes could not be depended on to complete the most minute task, including closing a car door. He simply did not remember to. The bedwetting continued. At this age, I had serious doubts that he would grow out of any of it. I feared that these kinds of problems, if they persisted as he went into adolescence, would psychologically damage him, if they had not already. The seriousness of not being able to trust Weston with responsibility had not yet hit me. The potential danger to him was always in my mind, however. I felt he would have to be protected no matter what age he was.

Wes proved to be accident prone more and more as he grew physically. I dreaded knowing he was off alone, around water, crossing a street, using a knife, etc. Certainly, he was too old for such dread and apprehension! But Wes was different.

That year, his fifth grade teacher suggested, and later insisted, that he be examined by an outside professional. She gave me the name of a doctor in a town forty-five minutes from home. I used all sorts of arguments against it but finally gave in.

CHAPTER 9
*(Written September 1984)

As I sat in the corner of the small examining room watching the doctor take hold of my son's toes, one by one, my mouth fell open in dumbfounded surprise. The test was an easy, painless one. Wes was lying down on the examining table and could not see what the doctor was doing. Calmly, and without any reaction whatever, the doctor would ask, "Which toe am I holding onto, Weston?" Then, he would ask, "Which way am I moving your toe, up or down?"

A simple test, an astounding revelation! My son could not identify the toe being clasped or the direction in which it was being moved. Actually, if what he tried to tell the doctor had been fact, he would have had seven toes on his right foot! He could not tell right from left, and he had "small" and "large" confused.

Weston not only does not have seven toes but no visible signs of abnormality. He is outwardly in almost every way a normal ten year old. Physically, he is tall, and although he is very thin, he has strong, handsome features. He is a red-headed, sweet, introverted child whose real problem he related to the doctor: "I just can't remember." The doctor, observing my child for the first time, immediately zeroed in on Wes' problems as soon as we were alone together.

What Wes did have and has had since birth was MBD (Minimal Brain Dysfunction)|now termed ADD(Attention Deficit Disorder)|. He is, I was told by the doctor, one of nearly eight million children, the majority of which are males, making their way through a confused, disorderly life and an extremely difficult school career caused by a chemical imbalance in the brain. Upon learning this, I looked back on the denial which helped me build a wall of refusal that anything was permanently wrong with my child.

When Wes' fifth grade teacher suggested I have him evaluated by a child psychologist, I tried to hide my hurt and resentment. I felt she had to be wrong; she did not understand my child's problems; she did not care enough to take time with him. How wrong I was! At that time, I did have a terrible nagging fear that something was wrong, but I attributed it to other factors. To my utter dismay, my family, too, wholeheartedly agreed with his teacher! He needed evaluation. Even my sister Jan, who was dying with cancer in the hospital that spring of 1983, whispered quietly to me, "Kathy, it is the right thing to do. We have always known it."

I felt desperate for support. Being divorced, I believed, compounded my frustration. My divorce had caused Weston's problems for years: the late toilet training, the rocking, the slowness to learn to ride his bicycle. So many times I thought, "What have we done to our child?" His father never took time with him, but then, I worked away from home constantly, too. Feelings of guilt overwhelmed me.

Suddenly, I was forced to acknowledge what I had feared in the back of my mind each new school year since the kindergarten teacher wanted to have Wes "held back." He needed so much help. My family did not want to say, but they had held this belief for years. Why? I was a miserable failure as a mother. Fears assailed me. The psychologist will accuse me of neglect. It was true that I had built a successful career for myself which required extensive travel. Perhaps Wes was subconsciously refusing to "grow up."

For all his sweetness, he would not cooperate at home, he would not help by helping himself, and worst of all, he would not let me or anyone else physically hug him or kiss his cheek. I hoped and prayed daily that all of this aversion and resistance to physical affection would disappear with maturity.

Wes was not outgrowing his problems, however. Physical maturity intensified everyone's criticism of the symptoms that were being manifested by the yet untreated MBD. For the first time, Wes complained that the other children made fun of him. He didn't fit in. He could not find his place. He couldn't remember to close a door behind him. He was said to be "dreaming" in school. He forgot and forgot and forgot. So many repeated instructions and reminders went unheeded in our daily lives that I sounded like a tape recording.

Homework was a nightmare, starting at 7:00 p.m. and ending maybe by 11:00 p.m. This was only when he managed to get home with his assignments at all! If I did not monitor his work at home, he brought home countless incomplete papers marked with D's and F's. Little did I know that his teachers were going through the same problems at school, only much worse. He could not stay seated at his desk. He was constantly looking for something among his things. He made strange sounds that bothered the other children. He began a test or other assignment only to trail off into a little world of his own and never finish unless prodded continuously. With all these complaints, there were contradictions: He could learn, he could read and spell, and he could make extraordinary speculations for a child his age on life and things that interested him. He seemed very bright!

His fifth grade teacher was patient and dedicated, but more importantly, she was alerted to the symptoms that plague an MBD [ADD] child. This teacher, in a small, rural private school was informed and felt a responsibility. Because she recognized what was happening to Weston was not deliberate or due to lack of intelligence or interest, but actually a physical problem, Weston's life is different today. She saw the facial twitches, the lost and confused look in his eyes when confronted with something that he had not (but should have) easily remembered. She saw the lack of motor control and clumsy tripping and falling about. She saw a healthy ten year old who shunned boys his own age to play with younger children on the playground. She saw the distorted, uncontrolled handwriting that would not write the answers that she was sure he knew so well.

In the nearly two hours of frank discussion with the doctor, I managed to get all of my fears out into the open. He was outwardly bemused by my agitation, but in a kindly way. Very gently he announced to me that Weston was now, and has always been, functioning in this world at a real disadvantage. It had nothing to do with having a divorce, being an overprotective mother, or a distant father. He questioned me carefully, and each answer seemed to confirm his "diagnosis."

Wes had a hereditary minimal brain dysfunction, treatable with one tiny pill (Imipramine) at night before bed. MBD can be dramatically reversed, and hyperkinetic symptoms are all but erased. The drug would enable Weston, like so many others with similar problems, to do the things that we take for granted in our children's maturation process. He will remember instructions; he will sit down and eat quietly with other children; he will have an attention span appropriate for his age; he will place time in proper sequence; he will catch a ball! And he did do all these things—and more! He was one of the very few children to memorize all of the books of the Bible that early summer in Bible School. The noises and twitches disappeared.

The one problem? We did not know what the proper dosage would be for Wes or when was the best time for him to take it. It was "hit or miss" at first. He couldn't have too much or it would put him to sleep in school, but he had to have enough to do what it was supposed to do. Regulating the proper dosage in an active, growing boy would certainly be a challenge and a serious responsibility.

I did not know then, but have wondered since, if the little pill could have corrected all of the symptoms that now I realize are characteristics of MBD (or ADD) children: the catatonic bouncing; the confusion about body parts and extreme modesty; slow speech; crying and broken speech patterns; chronic, prolonged bedwetting; late developing motor skills (riding a bicycle); a high frustration level; and failure in school when the child is obviously bright.

My son can take messages on the telephone; before, he would not even answer it. His report cards bear testimony to this little miracle drug. Weston makes nearly all A's and B's!

Teachers and neighbors praise his behavior now, when in the past he had been asked not to participate in a certain school function or not to return to a neighbor's home. All of these things have changed our lives so much that it is strange now to look back and think of how we lived with Wes before the little tablet we call "the memory pill."

His fifth grade teacher wrote me the following letter, which I copied and sent to the doctor:

"The improvement in Weston's classroom and play-ground behavior is remarkable. He is a totally different student. The frustrations he has shown in playground and classroom behavior is no longer evident.

In the classroom Weston is able to complete his assignments very quickly and with little effort on my part to keep him quiet. He is eager to ask for help and asks very intelligent questions. The noises and walking he once did have declined greatly. I don't expect any student to be perfectly still and quiet all the time. He is more normal for the level now. No longer is he disorganized and so messy. The handwriting is so much improved.

His lunchroom behavior has had a drastic improvement. Weston can sit quietly and eat without making a mess all around him or on himself. He also finishes his lunch in a reasonable length of time because he doesn't play as he eats.

On the playground I can see that Weston is beginning to participate in the older kids' activities. They seem to be accepting him better in the things they do. This is also evident in our P. E. activities, because they are encouraging him. This could be because his coordination seems some better.

There are so many little things which are improving in Weston. Some are so subtle that I really don't realize them until asked and look back over the chart I checked earlier. I find myself really wanting to encourage him to do more and more. When shown his mistakes, he really wants to do it right. Weston is very obviously intelligent, and it should be more and more evident.

One area that I feel Weston has shown his greatest improvement is testing. All items seem to be easier for him to complete, even the "fill in the blank" or "answer in a sentence." Before I would read these to him after reading them to the class. He doesn't ask to have them explained nearly as often. His grades have really improved.

If I should sound excited about Weston—I am. I only wish we, as teachers, could reach each child and help him as you have with Weston. It makes our jobs so much easier and more rewarding."

There is a difference in our attitudes, feelings, and daily routines, even though Wes still has his bad days. His sister, Shea, is much more patient with him, and as his "second little mother," her burdens have been eased. All who know him see the remarkable change. Though he is still a little different, that only makes him more special. For all of this I am grateful, but there was one special blessing I had not counted on. This was the day I came home from a business trip and went to hug his usually limp unresponsive body to me in greeting. He opened his arms to me and actually hugged me back!

"Hello, Mom," he said. "I'm glad you're back."

At that moment, it was as if my little ten year old boy had taken a long trip away, but now he was back.

*The above was written in September 1984 after Wes had been taking his "memory pill" for several months. I thought everything was going to be all right because he seemed on the road to normalcy—thanks to this "miracle" medication. How wrong I was! I had no way of knowing what the side effects of the medicine were nor what was to happen several years later.

CHAPTER 10

May 3, 1983, we drove in a four-hour funeral procession on a beautiful spring day to the cemetery in my home town. Six long, horrifying, sad months had passed while we watched Jan, then thirty-four years of age, slowly succumb to cancer. I had not known such strain or trauma since my divorce. My two children had been left almost constantly in the care of sitters and family members as I struggled to take on my fair share of the watch and work when I could. With all of the struggle, I bore a burden of guilt and never felt that I had done enough. When we all accepted that Jan's death was imminent, the strength from which we all drew to keep us going—hope—was ebbing away. I loved her so much. I could not imagine life without her.

Everyone was bone tired from the long drive when we arrived home. We were all relieved that the ordeal of watching Jan suffer was over but were filled with sadness and disbelief from this incredible tragedy. I grieved alone, not wanting my children to be affected as I was from her death. Once, when they saw me crying at the kitchen sink during breakfast, they both asked me anxiously what was wrong. I admitted that I was crying for Jan because I missed her but hastened to add that she was in a better place. I wanted not only to spare them from seeing me in pain but also from the realization that death changes our lives forever when it is the death of someone we love.

Shea and Wes had been neglected during Jan's illness and shuttled back and forth so long that I thought it my duty to get back as quickly as possible on an even keel. I wanted to indulge them and put some of myself back into their lives. Unfortunately, this did not include lessons on death and dying and how people handle grief.

The last time Shea and Wes saw their Aunt Jan, a vibrant live-life-to-the-fullest individual, was on Christmas Day. Then, she went back to Baton Rouge, deathly ill, though they did not know it. They were not prepared, counseled, or even confided in when things got worse and we knew there was no longer hope. I thought this was a way of sheltering them. In retrospect, I wish I had tried to explain to them how much death hurts those of us who are left behind and further, if I lost one of them, I would suffer greatly. I wish I had shared my grief with them and asked them their feelings about the loss of their aunt.

Wes and Shea had never been to a funeral. Rarely had they even seen a cemetery except from the outside gates. Jan's death was the first time they had experienced the effects of a death— the quiet gathering of friends and family, the ceremonious gathering at the casket, the floral offerings, the condolences, the teary eyes, the sadness. This went on for three days. Still, we all agreed that the children would all be with us and go to the funeral and the cemetery.

Jan's two young children who survived her would need their cousins around them. Weston and Jan's youngest son, Brown, were especially close. Brown, only seven at the time of his mother's death, was confused and hardly knew what was happening most of the time. He stuck close to ten-year-old Weston's side as we walked around the monuments toward the freshly dug mound of red clay that was to be Jan's grave. One of the vivid remembrances, now, after the poignance of our family's having to gather for such a sad occasion was how the little tow-headed boy recognized the spelling of his name, Brown, on many nearby gravestones. His was a family name which Jan had chosen for him. He asked Weston, in the trusting way that youthful curiosity can only be understood by another child, "Why is my name on all of these stones out here?"

Wes replied, "I don't know. You must have been out here before sometimes."

After my sister's death, my brother-in-law remarried. His new wife had a son close to Brown's age who was totally opposite from my sister's child. He was quiet, manageable, and withdrawn from people.

My nephew was a reflection of Jan's "never-meet-a-stranger" personality. Brown was vibrant and mischievous; he already excelled in school and abounded with athletic ability. He was active but showed no other problems.

When my brother-in-law called me with great concern, knowing that Weston was now taking medication and asking questions about it, I reassured him. After all, I would like the idea of Wes' having company in this battle against "undesirable traits." However, it bothered me that Jan had advised me to take Wes for evaluation, but she saw no problem with her own child. Like me, she had been a school teacher for over ten years. Was it just that Brown's step-mother wanted an easier adjustment with him? Only a few months later she and my brother-in-law divorced, and Brown never took medication again.

CHAPTER 11

We embarked on Wes' sixth grade school year with the "memory pill." That fall, he was convinced by friends and coaches he should go out for football. Again, this was a disappointing endeavor. Other than the football experience, new and positive things happened. He got along well with the other boys his own age and made friends with more than a few. They shared many interests besides football. He seemed to be accepted and winning self-respect. He did very well in his subjects. Thanks to the little pill, the bedwetting had stopped, so he began to spend the night with his friends. His facial tics had completely disappeared, also.

Wes admired one boy in particular, a rough and tumble boy who liked mischief and fun. He spent the weekend with this boy once, and soon after we had a visit from the local juvenile officers. A complaint had been filed against two unidentified boys for ransacking an elderly man's deserted house and shooting it up with BB guns. Wes had taken his BB gun with him to spend the weekend with his friend because they were going to hunt blackbirds.

The officers and I sat in the den facing Weston. During the questioning I knew Wes was not telling the truth. He avoided looking straight at the officers and cleared his throat each time before answering a question. He was obviously frightened, but lying. Finally, I knew these men would not be in my home if they had no reason to suspect Weston, so I took him off to the kitchen alone to talk to him. Knowing how naive my son could be, I explained to him that they probably had fingerprints or evidence and that they would find out the truth one way or another. Wes seemed relieved to tell me the truth and get it off his chest. This was his first brush with the law at the tender

age of eleven, and he was anxious to have it over with. Together, Wes and I carried a check for the damages out to the old
man's family, and Wes apologized to them.

As we drove home, I chided my child one last time for
destruction of property, even if he thought the house was
abandoned, and also for following along behind friends who
thought it great fun to do something bad. The father of the friend
who had been with Wes was furious because Wes had let the
truth out. An ugly exchange of words passed between the father
and me. He let it be known that Wes was no longer welcome at
his house, and I thought it "good riddance" of a bad influence.

Now that Wes was attaining the status of being accepted
by boys his own age, I realized that this acceptance could bring
real trouble. He was so eager to be accepted that he was
vulnerable. Although he could discern the difference between
right and wrong, he was more inclined to just go along with
whatever happened. It was ironic that the incident of property
destruction resulted when Wes would have been all too happy
to shoot at blackbirds with his BB gun as planned. Why did
trouble begin to follow at the heels of my son? How did it lead
this gentle boy to self-destruction?

Wes joined the church and was baptized when he was
twelve years old. We seldom missed a Sunday in Sunday School
and church, and he frequently sat next to me in church. When he
was older, he sat down in front with his friends.

I stood at the kitchen sink and watched him throw a
basketball up at the goal over the garage door. Now and then
he would look back at the window to see if I noticed he had made
a goal. For the first time in his life, I was really worried about
his future. Things were going along all right, but I had a nagging feeling of foreboding which made me ponder the past difficulties and anticipate certain future difficulties.

The summer of Weston's thirteenth birthday, he tried
water skiing for the first time. He finally skied for a short time
right behind the boat but only after many frustrating tries. His
younger cousin, Brown, had mastered every water toy imagin-
able that lay on the huge ski barge. As a water skier myself, I

watched Weston's bent awkward form and wondered silently, "Why does everything always have to be so hard for him?" I knew from years of watching skiers come and go on the old lake that he would never sail gracefully past the floating barge filled with teenagers and throw water at everyone with the back of his ski.

Wes came back to the barge, proud of himself for what he had done, and vowed to no one in particular, as he paced back and forth, that next summer he would ski on one ski. He was enjoying the water now—diving, swimming, paddling boats, and of course, fishing. He never seemed to tire of it. This same boy who had been hyperactive in school could out fish, with enduring patience, even his grandfather. Together the two of them spent many quiet hours on the lake, floating and looking for bass or perch, talking only now and then. I was grateful for moments like these when his life was not filled with inner battles and self-defeating frustrations.

Wes spent a happy week in Florida that summer with his father. Shea was so busy with cheerleader camp and Girls State that she was unable to go on the trip. This gave Wes a rare chance to have all his dad's attention. He had an experience with the opposite sex during that week. He came back with a crush on a girl his age who had been there with her parents. He arranged pictures of the beach and ocean on his bulletin board in his room, replacing less important mementos and waited anxiously for a letter from his new friend. After a few weeks passed, it became apparent that Wes' father forgot to send him the girl's address. Another disappointment, but his first in matters of puppy love.

CHAPTER 12

In 1986, then fourteen and a high school freshman, Weston fell in love. Uncharacteristically, he could not hide his feelings. He picked up the telephone numerous times to dial the girl's number and would only put it down again. He talked about her and how he felt bad that she had been in a car accident. He wanted to do something special for her. It amazed me. Shortly before Christmas he sent me on an errand to buy a Swatch Watch for this girl. The faddish watch was a prized possession at the time for any teenager. He waited anxiously for my arrival with the watch. He looked at it and approved my selection. Then he agonized over the words to write on the card that would accompany the gift and convey his feelings along with it. His very astute sister and older girl cousin, Hope, in their "knowing ways" about "these things," let him know he was being a fool. However, nothing deterred him. After numerous attempts, he closed the final card and caught a ride with a friend to take the gift and card over to her house. He waited for her response. None was given, not even a "thank you."

The whole experience was a blow for Wes, but I felt (and hoped) that he had recovered and realized that sometimes feelings like his were not returned in kind. He knew nothing about girls, and his hurt was aggravated by some teasing he endured. The inevitable "I told you so!" came from his sister and cousin who disliked the girl. They were indignant that he set himself up for a fall with one who so obviously didn't deserve his attentions.

Christmas 1986 came and went. It was a good Christmas. Weston got a screen for his computer. He loved to play computer games and put in hours with it. He became interested in new

clothes and shoes in the latest styles. He was growing tall and
filling out. I saw a young man blossoming beneath the adolescent awkwardness. He developed a deep voice. A new personality emerged. But that personality was angry.

The weather turned cold and gray. Snow was being fore-
cast. Wes, as usual, got excited and went to ready the ingredients
for snow ice cream. This action was more like the little boy I
was familiar with.

Snow didn't come, though. Every disappointment such as
this one made me hurt for him. His mood swings increased.

Spring had not arrived, but the warming weather spurred
excitement, anticipation of more activity, and contemplation of
mischief by bored youths in the community. They wandered
about trying to act older than they were.

Wes was one of them. He dressed to the hilt and went out
to do nothing. The teenagers began drinking in private gather-
ings. They devised ways to get out of the house just to talk
and drink, these over-young boys who were too new to girls and
too old for toys.

Uneasiness about Weston dominated my thoughts during
this time, even when he was right under my nose. My work
weeks were long and hard. Yielding under the pressures of work
and troubling problems with Wes, I curtailed my own social life
to be home with him and Shea, who would be graduating from
high school that May. I wanted to be there with them both as
much as possible and still devote more time to work to increase
sales commissions to make more money for Shea's college ex-
penses.

One April night in 1987, Wes and his friends went camping. He had been grounded for an incident involving alcohol the
weekend before, and I made him promise he would *not* do two
things if he were allowed to go: drink or leave the campsite in
a car.

Just to put my mind at ease before I went to bed that night,
I drove out to the tent I had given him the Christmas before last.
I shined my lights on it to reassure myself that he was there. I
did not call him out to the car and risk embarrassing him by re-

minding him of his promise. Satisfied that he was there, I turned the car around and drove back home.

At two o'clock the phone next to my bed rang.

"Mrs. Sandefer, do you have a son named Wes?" No one in
town called me Mrs. Sandefer. I knew something was wrong.

"Yes," I answered, groggily.

"You need to come down to the courthouse. He has been in
a wreck."

"But it can't be Wes! He's camping," I said, denying the
realization that this must be the materialization of all the bad
feelings I had been having.

"He was with two other friends. They were drinking. You
better come down right away."

"But, is he hurt? Is he all right?"

"He'll probably need to go to the clinic, but he seems okay."

I hung up the telephone and hurriedly dressed in a fog of
fear and apprehension. It couldn't be that bad or they would
have come to get me instead of calling. I told myself to just be
calm and hold on to my emotions. He would be all right.

The courthouse was closed and dark. I became aware of
blinking lights, reflecting in the trees across the street. As I
walked around to the other side of the building, I heard running
steps behind me. I turned to see the mother and father of
Weston's best friend. Wes had been camping with their son.
They were hurrying forward with fear in their eyes. Then we
saw the fire truck and overturned car. The mother screamed and
grabbed the arm of her husband. My knees went limp, but I
made my legs run while I sought a glimpse of my child. Wes
stepped out of the back of a police car and into my arms. He buried his bloody face in the shoulder of my coat, but said nothing. I
silently thanked God he was alive and just held him tightly,
not asking any questions.

The police officers accompanied us to the local clinic where
the boys were X-rayed and treated. Wes required stitches in his
leg for a puncture wound. The other two boys were miraculously
unharmed except for bumps and bruises.

The police wanted to question the boys before releasing

them. They told us about the damage that had been done to the airport runway lights. Two lights were found in the back seat of the wrecked car, so they knew that Wes and his friends had destroyed the others. I listened incredulously. I kept thinking, "We can get past this. He is all right. He is all right!"

It was early morning by the time the two of us reached home. Wes was so stunned by the night's events that he could hardly talk anymore about it. He said very quietly as we pulled into the carport, "I learned a lesson tonight. We could have been killed."

CHAPTER 13

Wes was not doing well in school. His grades the semester before Christmas had been excellent. Then he rebelled against his medication. His grades plummeted. Even before the report cards were out, I knew he hadn't fared well that six weeks. In anger and frustration, I went into his bedroom to try to explain to him exactly what MBD was, what little I knew or understood about his problem, and what we were trying to deal with. He coldly stared at me. I was so frustrated and tired of it all, I just simply didn't know what to do.

"Mom, I'm all right!" He took me by the shoulders, my son who rarely ever touched me. He turned me around to face him. "I can do it without that pill!"

I looked up at him and realized how tall he had grown. I didn't know what to do when I heard the pleading in his voice.

"You don't even know what it does!" he continued.

I didn't know. He had been on medication for nearly four years—one kind of pill or another. What were the long term effects? I wondered when he would be able to function without them. Maybe he deserved a chance to wean himself away.

I went to school to visit each of his teachers and tried for the first time to make an appeal to them to try to understand that Wes was under a strain due to a "medical" problem and might need help. Most of them clearly did not know what I was talking about nor why it mattered!

Even though I told Wes that I thought he needed to continue taking the medicine to do well in school, I called the doctor. I had misgivings about whether the medicine was safe and also because I was haunted by Wes' unhappiness. I wished as much as Weston did that I would be told that the time had come to cease the pills. I related these feelings to the doctor. He was not encouraging. He suggested that I bring Weston in for a consultation. I knew the only way to get Wes back to the doctor was to trick him. We were going shopping for some new clothes for him, but on the way I broke the news that I intended to take him to the doctor first. He became upset but did not put up as big a battle as I had anticipated. I think he really wasn't sure himself what course he wanted to take but was afraid of being talked into continuing the pills. That is exactly what happened. After about a half hour visit, Weston emerged with the doctor, and they shook hands. The doctor informed me, as the three of us stood together, that he and Wes had come to an agreement. Wes would only take a small Ritalin tablet once in the morning on school days. His friends need not know about it. He could have his weekends off of the medication. Wes was calm and stared down at the floor as the doctor talked.

This was the first time Ritalin had been used in regard to Weston's treatment. I hated the word. There was so much controversy surrounding it. I did not believe Weston's treatment called for the use of Ritalin and had been pleased that it had not been used before. I did not know what to expect from Ritalin.

In the car Wes was not distressed so much as resigned. He seemed as tired of the whole business as I was. I took him to buy the clothes I had promised him before we went to the doctor's office. I also bought him two new pairs of leather shoes in styles highly craved by boys his age. I was rewarding him as we traditionally did for a "good" doctor's visit, but was I buying his forgiveness? We went to fill the prescription for Ritalin, and I tried to put the outcome of his disastrous experiment of going without medication behind us.

Not long after that, Shea confronted me in the kitchen as I wearily unloaded groceries from the car with, "Mom, I'm worried about Wes. He's drinking all the time."

I knew I wasn't up to dealing with another crisis, so I skirted the issue. "That can't be. Where would he be getting it?"

"They are all getting it," she said, disgustedly, and left.

Report cards for the next six weeks came out. I had not

yet seen Weston's. Shea's graduation parties were in full swing in April already, and I had planned a crawfish boil for her and her cousin Hope out on the lake. The party was that Friday night . . . no time to worry about Wes' grades right then.

I had been working non-stop because the spring weather had been good for traveling after the cold winter months, and time was racing by. This was Shea's time. For once in her life, this was going to be Shea's special time. I decided to just concentrate on the party.

Walking into the den, I noticed a note written in red ink lying on the table. It had been written by the school principal to Weston's math teacher. In it, the principal assured her that he would suspend Wes for three days for the disruption he had caused in her class.

I confronted Wes, who was watching TV. He shrugged it off, saying it was only an in-school suspension which meant he had to stay in the principal's office. Besides, he continued, he wasn't the only one involved. He was in a foul mood and wanted to avoid a confrontation. I had no time, anyway. The party for Shea was that night.

Wes informed me that he did not want to go to the lake for Shea's party. He said he had made plans to play golf with a friend that afternoon and that they might drive down later. He knew such an arrangement, after all I have been through with him, would not be acceptable. He chanced it, though. Angrily, I called the friend to confirm his plans and was told that no such plans were made. To think that he would cause problems the night of Shea's graduation party really aggravated me. I accused him of lying so he could stay in town and get into trouble. After a loud argument, he finally gave up and got into the car with me to go to the party. Shea had gone on ahead to help with the preparations.

Alone in the car with Wes, we had an unpleasant talk on the way to the lake. I was totally confused by his behavior and the feeling that I could not trust him. If only I knew how to reach him!

Recently, I had made a telephone call to his father asking

for help and support with Wes. Rick came and took Wes home with him for the weekend. Desperately searching for some kind of help for my son, I suggested to Weston while we drove to the lake that he might want to go stay with his father for a while, although I knew it would tear my heart out. He did not respond. The talk led to an argument. I told him I knew about the drinking that had been going on. He denied it, and I accused him of lying. So emphatic was I that he realize how serious this was that I told him, "I can never allow you to drive if you are going to drink."

Wes became upset and said, "Mom, I'll do anything if you will just let me drive."

Then I realized how preposterous my threat was because he had not even been able to learn how to drive, with all the coordination problems he had, although he continued to try. However, mastering the skills of driving seemed far beyond his capabilities. When would these problems ever end? How could I solve any of them?

Anger compounded the frustration, and we both fell into despondent silence. I drove without saying anything. I thought about the report card that was due out and the possibility of failing grades. Suddenly, I turned to Wes and said that if he failed at the private school he was attending, he was not going to the local public high school next year. He knew I meant what I said. (I had no way of knowing that he had already gotten failing grades, and my statement dashed his hopes of changing to the public high school. He had hidden his report card from me. Sometime during that past six weeks, he told his cousin Hope that I thought he was taking his pills, but he wasn't. The result was failing grades in two subjects.) Now, I know that his depression had to have contributed to the failing grades, and he was probably thinking of suicide that very moment.

Finally, we reached the lake. Wes was very upset. He furiously got out of the car. I went about giving the party and Wes, too young for the graduating seniors gathered there, fell in with the other kids. We were on a collision course for disaster, and I was having a party!

Busy with seeing about the food and looking after teenagers running around the grounds, I forgot about Weston's problems and the argument. Two hours later, however, Shea came up to me and blurted out that Wes was drunk and embarrassing her. I quickly went to see for myself, and sure enough, he was.

Wes resisted being put to bed, but since we were planning to stay overnight, I thought it best to get him settled and away from the others who were obviously drinking, too. Alcohol was never served at these senior parties, but many brought their own liquor and beer, drinking it around the cars in the darkness. Weston had been downing what he could from glasses, cups, and bottles that were set down.

No sooner had I gone back to where the other adults were boiling crawfish and vegetables and started tending the fire when Wes burst through the screened door of the camp and fell to his knees in the grass, vomiting violently.

No explanation to anyone was needed. I put my son into the car and drove straight for home. He was so sick that I feared alcohol poisoning. I had to stop along the roadside more than once. I finally reached home and helped him into bed; I watched him throughout the night. Worry, exhaustion, and fear plagued me.

The next day, Saturday, May 2, Weston seemed in good spirits. He laughed and smiled most of the afternoon. He ate and played. He mowed part of the yard, promising to finish it the next day. He carried a Sony Walkman with him on the lawnmower. He had taped just four songs which he played over and over.

Early that night, Wes came to the door of my bathroom, my private domain in the back of the house where I sometimes shut myself off from the world. "Mom?" he said.

I asked, "What is it, Wes?"

"Nothing," he said and walked away.

A few minutes later I found him outside in the darkness. He came in and sat beside me on the couch. We looked through his new high school annual. He had gotten one of his own for the first time that year. I found his class picture and remarked that he was the best looking boy on the page. He smirked and looked away. When I asked if there were any other pictures of him anywhere in the annual, he said disgustedly, "No," and started watching TV.

I was going out for the evening with the man I had been seeing for about three years. Just before we left about nine, Wes said for me not to worry about him. "I'll be all right," he said. I told him I would call to check on him, and I'd be home about 11:30.

The telephone at the Country Club where we went was out of order, so I was unable to call home to Wes. I was home shortly before 11:30. All the lights in the house and the garage were on. The TV was on, and the dog was sitting in the living room. There was a freshly eaten bowl of chocolate ice cream on a table. I expected to find Wes up watching television. I went to his bedroom to see if he had gone to bed. His bedroom door was locked.

I knocked on the door and called his name. I knew he was probably sleeping or had "sneaked" out of the house for a quick jaunt around the neighborhood—a prank that many of his fourteen-year-old friends had begun to play. I decided to force the lock, not really expecting to find him in his bedroom. I did not feel overly concerned because I knew if he were not there, he wouldn't be far away.

When I opened the door, I saw him lying there on the bedroom floor. I saw the blood . . . so much blood around his head! The room was covered with a spray of blood. I screamed and ran to him. His hands were drawn up toward his body like a small dead bird's claws. His eyes were open and staring. At that moment I knew he must be dead. His eyes wouldn't be open like that if he were asleep. The shock was too severe to cause fainting. Spears of awareness assaulted every cell in my body; I was totally alert. I reached out to touch his auburn hair. I think I called his name. When I went to brush his hair back, my eyes caught sight of something so horrible . . . His brains were visible behind his head. I quickly drew away and screamed in terror, "Someone has killed him!" I felt invaded. Real fear that the murderer still lurked in the house filled my mind with terror.

Hands were pulling me from the room. I couldn't look at anyone, see anything but Weston.

By now, I saw my son was irreversibly destroyed . . . beyond repair. I reeled down the hallway screaming and trying with all of my might to go out of my mind, to lose consciousness, to die. Anything would have been merciful.

I saw the faces of my brother and sister-in-law, rushing toward me. I ran into their arms, but I couldn't look at them.

Someone called the police on the telephone. "Come quick! Wes is dead!"

I kept crying out, "Don't say that! Oh, don't say he is dead!"

Someone's hands and arms were holding me up. Somebody continued talking to me, even though I repeatedly said I didn't want to hear.

I tore my way outside and knelt down in the grass on the lawn and prayed to almighty God that He had to stop this nightmare. He had to help me. I told God I could not make it without His help. I kept repeating, "How can I live with this? How will I ever be able to live with this?" I asked Him to remove the memory of what I had just seen from my mind forever. I alternately prayed for Him to take away the horror from my mind and cried, "Why? Why?" over and over again.

Voices that went with the hands and arms were telling me that my son had killed himself with his own shotgun. The force of the discharge had thrown it under the bed. I didn't want to hear that my son whom I had loved and protected from harm for fourteen years, soon to be fifteen, had taken his own life! He wouldn't do something like that! He had not left a message for me, had not even said goodbye except to tell me when I left home earlier that evening that he would be "all right."

Now, our driveway was lined with police cars with lights flashing. People were going in and out of my home at an hour when we should have been asleep in bed. I realized even then that with that shotgun blast, our lives were forever blown apart and not only could we not go to bed, I could never come back to this house again. I would never see Weston alive again.

All night long I cried, "How will I ever live with this?" The onslaught of crushing pain was almost unbearable.

But morning came. It was Sunday. I asked my brother for a Bible like a drowning person seeking a nearby arm or tree to grab onto. It suddenly entered my mind that if anything might suppress my screams of agony, my hysterical crying, my Bible could. I knew God would help me because He had already allowed me to live through a night I thought I would not be able to survive and didn't want to.

I first prayed for God to let me be dreaming and to wake me up from this terrible nightmare. But no. This was real! God did not wake me up. Weston had chosen to die. He was no longer with us.

I asked the funeral director if he would cut a lock of Weston's hair for me, so I could remember its beautiful auburn color. Secretly, I wanted him to prove to me that my son was really in that casket and not lying somewhere in a laboratory still being autopsied, a mandatory law in the state after a violent death. The casket was never opened. No one saw Weston again.

The funeral was delayed until Monday afternoon, May 4, but that was not near long enough for me. I did not want a funeral. How could I face this, too? Operating on wired nerves and throat-constricting spasms of mourning when I would dare let myself look into the future without him, I forced myself to make decisions about a casket, his clothes, and a private graveside service. I did not want people who were not close to me to see me. I was afraid—afraid that even after God had told me He would give me strength, I would lose control.

I was numb most of the service and cried inwardly. I could hear Weston's father weeping aloud. Strangely, it did not move me. Shea and I sat clutching each other's hands without a word, staring at the blue coffin in which rested the body of our beloved Wes, whom we had lived, laughed, cried, and struggled with for over fourteen years. Nothing seemed real.

After the service, my mother said to me, "It's all right to cry now." But I couldn't cry. It would not have been possible to cry hard enough or moan loud enough with as great a sorrow as I felt at that time, so I did not even try.

It wasn't until two weeks had passed that the hysterical crying began. I went about the mechanics of living, getting dressed, appointing myself some task at hand, writing notes to those who had brought food or flowers, helping Shea with her graduation invitations, going back and forth to the cemetery. But I was just going through the motions of being in this world. My thoughts and my whole being were somewhere with Weston—before the suicide, during the suicide, after the suicide, in Heaven. Where was my child? When would I see him again? I needed to see him!

Shea and I had been staying at my brother's home since the night of the tragedy. He and my sister-in-law had returned to their home in Tulsa by now. Everyone agreed that it was best, and as far as they were concerned, we should never go back home, but I knew I would go back. I felt compelled to go back to the bedroom where I had discovered his body.

I forced through my brain several times a day a mental exercise of remembering the way Weston had looked and how everything in the room had looked that night, so I could get used to it. I didn't want the door at the end of the hallway to hold some ominous dread for me. The room in which my son lived and died would not forever be a lingering tomb whose secrets were forbidden to me if I could help it.

The first time I opened the door to his room and looked in, I did not have the sensation of remembering the night of the suicide at all. It was the memory of the room he had lived in for seven years. Sunlight flooded in through the uncovered windows. Everything was gone—the carpet, the beds, the lamp, the things that hung on the wall, the toys, the pillows, the dresser, the curtains, the shoes and clothes. Everything . . . gone!

He's gone. It's all gone. Life with Weston, his room, his things, his teenage years, his future . . . gone! I fell down to my knees, holding onto the doorknob, and began to scream as hard as is physically possible until my throat went hoarse. No one heard; no one came. I didn't care. I was inconsolable.

CHAPTER 14

I turned to God in my deepest and darkest despair. The time had come in my life when I found that I needed Him more than anyone else. Not my mother, my father, my sister, my brother, or my daughter, although all were there for me. I just needed God.

By the end of the week after Weston was buried, I was seeking every shred of information, every reason from anywhere, desperate to know how and why this tragedy happened. I began the long quest for answers on which every survivor must embark. I listened to the tape he had in the Sony Walkman. Two of the four songs were "Don't Try Suicide" and "Save Me." I pondered every influence on my son which urged him on to his final destructive act.

Creativity many times comes out of emotional experiences. I poured out my thoughts on paper, sometimes sad offerings that were hidden away, not to be discussed with anyone, sometimes joyful remembrances of bygone days. I wrote poems, letters, notes to and about Wes, about myself, about anything, just to vent my emotions. Even though I will share some of these with you, I didn't really write them at the time to be shared with others, just to help ease my own pain and trauma. However, perhaps they will be of help to you or someone who has had a similar tragedy in their lives.

The following are some of the things I wrote during the first few months after the suicide.

May 5, 1987 (3 days after Weston's death)

When I was a girl, a freshman in college, we played a silly

game one night in the dormitory room. We played with a "Ouiji" board which was harmless fun unless, supposedly, the players were very superstitious or made the "Ouiji" convey evil messages.

Many questions passed through my mind when it came my turn to allow the pointed object to be mysteriously moved somehow in anticipation of fate. My question was, "What age will I be when I die?"

The plastic pointer was guided by lightly touching fingertips around and around the board. In our girlish imaginations it, seemingly, had a life of its own. The pointer stopped on the number 4 and then slowly moved over to 0.

"Oh," I thought, "so long a time left to live?"

The years passed one into another. So long a time left . . .

As my fortieth birthday approached, I thought back from time to time on that night, and although I knew my fate was not necessarily sealed by that foolish question and the answer that was given by the Ouiji board, I still had an uneasy feeling about being forty and passing into forty-one without some ubiquitous dread that I had played folly with my life.

So, with certain trepidations, I stepped into my fortieth year, not having the courage to tell a single soul about that night. Will I die? And how? Can I be so susceptible or even remotely preoccupied with death due to the prediction of just a stupid game? Wasn't I a Christian woman, trusting that God alone knew my fate and the plan of my life? Didn't I still have too much left to accomplish, too many responsibilities that I, and I alone, had to bear?

Then on the night of May 2 of the fortieth year of my life, my beloved only son took his life. When I found his poor, broken body, I did die at that moment. I died as only a mother can die when the life that came from her body ends, and she is left to live.

No matter how many more years the Lord has determined I will live, I know the Ouiji board's prediction was true: I died in part at age forty.

May 7, 1987

INADEQUATE WORDS

Sad cannot begin to describe the knowledge that your child did not want to live.

Horror cannot touch the realization that the broken body you kneel over is dead.

Disbelief is too pitiful a synonym for "How could this happen to us?"

Desperation may come lamely close to how it feels to tear your way back to sanity.

Dread is such a tiny little word for the fear that you may not be able to live with this.

Guilt is a simple name for "What could I or should I have tried to do to prevent this?"

Heartsick. How ridiculous it sounds when one is seeking a word to describe the pain inside the mind and body of a mother who must live with the endless regrets.

Anguish. Is that all that can be verbalized for the need to thrust your hand into the fresh mound of dirt on his grave?

Hope. So minuscule a word for the prayer that you and your remaining child can face the future and that she will be happy and sound with this tragedy marring her young years.

Comfort is only dimly descriptive for the feeling of taking the Bible on your lap to read God's words of peace and understanding.

Love is an overused four letter word. It is so inadequate for what you felt for him, what you feel for your daughter and family, what they feel for you. And what God is.

June 1, 1987

NOT FOREVER

"They say he killed himself."

That's what the gasoline station attendant said to my sister as I sat emotionless, as if invisible, on the passenger side.

"Were you any kin to that boy up there who killed hisself? Weren't that your nephew?"

"Yes, it was Kathy's son," she replied.

How could you explain to that poor old man, or anyone, that a fourteen-year-old boy who had an imagination rivaling a six year old really didn't want to kill himself. He just wanted to take himself out of life for a while because it was getting too troublesome, too confusing, too demanding, too hurtful, too fast. He wanted to let this painful time pass—but not forever.

I recalled after Wes' death that I had watched him amble through the house with his friends, all trying to impress each other, mostly ignoring me, kidding in an offhand manner, wandering aimlessly, nothing to do—not too many cares at all, it seemed. I had walked silently back to my bedroom and began to cry at the realization that my "little boy" was gone, never to be heard from or seen again because this strange teenager had taken over. But a brief walk outside or a close look inside his bedroom indicated "no," not completely gone. Tell-tale signs of immature imaginings were still there! Ropes tied on tree branches to broken pieces of a BB gun, small doll people hanging from the fence, carelessly constructed stick houses piled on the ground, and the amusing contortions he put his old stuffed animals through with shoestrings and toy handcuffs. Sometimes the little boy was still there. I remember asking him why he broke up his BB gun? Why did he play so violently with the doll people and just leave them stranded like that? Why did he mistreat his stuffed dog, "Le Mutt," so badly? He only laughed, a little embarrassed. I never pursued it too much. Now and then, I probably showed slight annoyance for having to remove the toys from under the lawnmower or the knots from the shoelaces. And of course, I didn't like for him to break things. My mild chastisings didn't stop him. He just continued playing.

In the same span of time, I began to ask him when he would get interested in something. He had a new computer, invitations to church activities, friends who showed interests in golf, tennis, and girls. Why not play with these boys who had more appropriate activities in mind for a boy soon to turn fifteen? I admitted to being somewhat disappointed to see friends his age at the Junior-Senior Prom that spring, but not my son. He said all the girls were "asked up." He showed no interest in these things. But I didn't really want to push him to grow up.

He had begun experimenting with alcohol and cigarettes, I knew, but never far from home. When one thing led to another after he became acquainted with beer and alcohol, he too-quickly discovered what could happen when a friend drinks and drives, exactly what the ads on TV and in magazines predicted. He really acted as if he were mentally shaken after the recent wreck. He seemed to understand that he was suddenly thrust into a non-pretend world where bad things could and did happen. I thought he would come around then. I thought he was growing up.

Withdrawal is so subtle. One doesn't have an opportunity to see things as they are portrayed in movies that center around problems like *Mask*. The red-haired gentle monster in those scenes was outwardly cheerful, inwardly dying. I had always known my young son well enough to know, however, that if something was on his mind, he was not able to concentrate on much of anything else: wanting a blue-jean jacket; having to have hightop Reebok tennis shoes; needing a Swatch Watch. Just so he would be "accepted" by his peers, and he had to have them THEN AND NOW! No waiting for Christmas or birthday. His instant happiness was my concern.

The gun? Well, that was proof-positive that he was loved and trusted. THE GUN. It was sentimental . . . having belonged to his paternal grandfather and given to him by his own father at Christmas. Of course, he was told not to keep it loaded—ever, and to stay away from the shells, as if they were dangerous without the gun. But with so much love attached to THE GUN, how could it hurt to let him have it now? He should have it in his room where he can see that he is so loved . . . and trusted.

When things didn't go well, he could handle the gun under his own power and authority, behind his locked bedroom door. When he got to thinking about those failing grades in school, he had THE GUN. After those getting-to-be frequent un-controlled drinking bouts with his too-young buddies, he had THE GUN. Thinking about taking medication to treat a so-called brain dysfunction (the something he couldn't even des-cribe that threatened to keep him from driving a car like the other guys at fifteen), not being able to excel in sports in high school, being ignored by the girl he paid such uncharacteristic attention to by giving her an extravagant gift, well, he had THE GUN. Then, the one thing that he was uniquely talented in, making his friends laugh, got him humiliated and suspended from class. All the trouble and the letting people down could be stepped away from if he wanted to . . . anytime he wanted to. He wouldn't be around. He had THE GUN!

Mr. Gasoline Station Attendant, it was as if he said to us all, "Life is pretty good, but it's confusing right now, so just let me leave for a while. I'll just hold my gun and think about it. It might be tonight. But first, I'll love my dog and watch some TV with him in our usual spot on the den couch. While I'm think-ing, I'll eat my ice cream with chocolate syrup as always. I think I'll walk outside and sit in the garage where Mom and I set up the weights for me to work out, but I'll still think about it. I'll visit my private hideout between the fences behind the garage; now I really feel pretty low. I'll go back to my bedroom and lock the door, get THE GUN down and think about it. I'll aim it a little toward myself—on my left side. I'll take the safety off this time; I'll stop the trouble, stop the frustration, stop the

feelings of being a failure and being different just for a little
while. Just for a while. But not forever.

No, mister, he didn't mean to kill himself . . . forever.

June 20, 1987

REQUIEM FOR A TEENAGE SUICIDE

If there has to be a question, then it surely would be, "Why?"
He did not want to tell us, or even say goodbye.

But there are other questions that logic would defy
To try and put a reason to if he were going to die.

Why would he need a haircut? His red hair would no
    longer grow.
Why would he save his money for where he was going to go?

Why would we buy the new spring clothes to fit his
    youthful frame,
Only now to buy a monument to bear his lonely name?

Why would he eat ice cream and cake and hotdogs
    on that day?
Was this a fitting last meal or a sign he'd go away?

Why would he want a new Swatch Watch so that he could
    tell the time,
If never seeing the future was what was on his mind?

If he planned to play the guitar, wouldn't he need to
    be around
To enjoy the learning of the chords, to listen to the sound?

Why will he have a birthday? July will be here in not
    too long,

But there won't be a fifteenth candle, and we won't
    sing the song.

Why did he suddenly stop his life, his struggle to survive?
Didn't he know that we'd have done anything to help
    him stay alive?

Was it for love and attention that was ever lacking here,
Or acceptance by his friends and peers that caused his
    dreadful fear?

No, I think he knew we loved him, and his friends were
    always there,
But confusion over many things had turned into despair.

So there must be a requiem for a teenage suicide.
A requiem is of peace and rest for someone who has died.

He must have sought the comfort that only God can give.
This poem is for my son, my boy, who did not want to live.

                         Kathleen Sandefer

I also read many books to ease my suffering. Some counselors would say to me, "I found it helpful to do this or that,"
and now looking back, I realize that there were things that did
help, if only for the moment.

Writing helped me vent the grief. Eventually, I found
there were support groups willing to listen. One of my greatest
helps was that offered by The Compassionate Friends, a national
support organization for bereaved parents and siblings. Their
newletters gave invaluable advice on how to handle the changes,
the holidays, the depression, and the emotional trauma that a
child's death brings.

CHAPTER 15

The softest warning whispered so often: "It will be hardest on holidays."

I remember looking forward to special days of the year when I was a little girl. I prepared for them mentally. When teachers wanted artwork produced—valentine boxes, Christmas trees, Easter egg dying—I never missed being a part of it. Looking forward to the day, the actual time in which everything would culminate, whether a Christmas morning, an Easter picnic, a birthday party, or the night of Halloween, made holidays longer for me.

As a teacher, I would decorate my classroom and allow the children special moments to create some memento of that season we were soon to celebrate with our families. As a mother, I collected pictures, ceramics, and candles for our home to commemorate the holiday. My two children responded by enjoying the preparations with me when they were old enough, and these times were sheer joy to me.

Weston died in May. I soon had to endure the first Mother's Day without my son. My sweet daughter remembered me with a card, and I set about the task of accepting that no day such as this would ever be the same, just as Father's Day had forever changed for them.

Summer was there before I knew it. The Fourth of July loomed ahead. My birthday, July 2, was always included in the festivities. This year, I lay in the bed with my head covered while my family courageously carried on. Each member urged me to join in the cookout planned at our camp on the lake. I was paralyzed with grief. I resented them for trying to make me forget that Wes was not there with us. How could they?

July 10, 1987 (Weston's birthday)

He has killed me. Oh, how it hurts. Real breathtaking pain. To know that he spent his last moments in such despair and confusion. To die alone, with no words of comfort to help, without my arms around him. Oh, God, how I wanted to protect him from this pain! How I tried, helplessly turning here and there, never knowing how he really felt about himself. He would say nothing. He was so brave but unable to face such utter defeat. No hope.

He has left me. After two long, unbearable months, I refuse to let him go. Oh, how I looked for him everywhere, in everything, frantically, desperately searching for a message left to me, or us, to tell me WHY. To tell anything! I suffer because he suffered, but now I suffer still.

He has broken up our tiny little family. He has ended the joys in the three of us together. Just building a fire, eating our favorite meals, planning our special family get-togethers, vacations. All ended. There were never enough times to be close, to share days that stood out from all the rest. The movies we watched, playing with our dog, Ling, the puzzles and games, all the things we loved together—all gone from us. Gone forever.

And Christmas. Oh, how I dread facing it ever again! I am so grieved and so afraid. I cannot let Shea down. I cannot burden my family. I cannot let them know that I want to stop the holidays. I cannot let them know how it hurts.

I can never tell anyone, especially my family, how it hurts that they do not seem as grieved as I do, to know that they will not grieve as long as I will for the loss of him. He will be forgotten. This is what I feel everyone wants to do but me. I am not allowed to look or feel sad. I am not allowed to make them sad. I am to forget. An unspoken agreement.

I don't want to be sad, so why should I wish this on the ones I love so dearly? They have been through so much. We have all been through so much together. But it is not fair that Weston's name should never be spoken because he is dead. If I say his name, there is anxious, awkward silence. No response. I cannot

get through to anyone that he is not dead to me. Why must I
discuss the living children in our family and never again mention my son because he is gone. It is so hard . . . so hard to be
unselfish.

I know that beyond my own hurt, he has hurt and angered
his sister. She did not go with me to the cemetery for his fifteenth birthday. Shea is the one living being that I cling to,
but I must not hold on too tightly. I will try not to make my
emotions burden her. She does not deserve anymore pain or
damage from this tragic nightmare. We do not speak of it
anymore. We loved him. Knowing that we loved him is all that
is left of him in our lives. It is over. Weston is home now, with
God.

July 1987

Strange that I should go all the way to Nashville, Tennessee
to find out that there was a support organization for survivors
close to my home in Louisiana. I had started back to work, work
which demanded staying in lonely hotel rooms at night but also
now demanded trying to contend with my grief as well. Even
after two months, I found myself unable to deal with the turmoil
that my life was in.

I boarded airplanes and felt that I was invisible to the other
passengers, but on at least two occasions, for some inexplicable
reason, I found myself pouring out my story to complete strangers. I was a wreck. The only thing that I found helpful was
writing. I wrote poems, recollections, stories. I also clipped and
copied articles concerning troubled children. I collected suicide
stories and bought books written for the bereaved. The particular problems that caused my son to suffer and feel such despair
were now paramount in my mind, and I read and reread material about Wes' MBD.

In the small rural community where I was from, there is
very little understanding of teenage suicide. This tragedy set
the entire town on edge, and then one week later, another fifteen year old boy followed Weston's example. I admit I dreaded

that Weston's suicide would be copied, but I found some comfort in the knowledge that this boy had both of his parents at home with him at the time; yet, it still made no difference. I was grasping at anything, even the circumstances of another child's death to assuage my feelings of guilt.

I had convicted myself for every single thing I had neglected doing to prevent Weston's death, even the fact that I was not at home and had gone out for the evening. There was no merciful release from any of the guilt before one more omission of duty was added to the list. I would not allow myself any relief. I went over and over in my mind the ordinary details surrounding the night of Weston's death.

He had talked to his best friend on the telephone that night and told him, "I guess I'm going to have to kill myself." And he had laughed.

I replayed the events countless times as I knew them to have occurred before the night of the suicide: the fact that he had written in friends' school annuals to take care of themselves because he "wouldn't be around to help them out of trouble"; the note from the principal; the missing report card; the argument we had; the visit to the doctor; the visit with his father; the graduation party which ended in disaster; and, the last day. I relentlessly picked through each detail, searching for any clue I had missed that could have helped me save his life.

Of course, not one young friend mentioned the suicidal messages in the annuals or the telephone call until after his death. His doctor didn't tell me he knew there were dangerous side effects to the medicine Wes was taking until after his death. His father asked me what had happened. The hints and warnings seemed to have escaped everyone, and they seemed reconciled to this, but I could not forgive myself for what happened.

The method of the suicide, the death scene—these are not the haunting, torturing fragments left with the suicide survivor. What is left are feelings of guilt and the questions: What really made him take his life? Was it my fault because of something I did or didn't do?

I loved him, and I must be exonerated. I don't know what really made Wes take his own life, but I have some pretty clear ideas. I could see the things that were making him miserable: problems in school; the difficulty in learning how to drive; the lack of confidence and inability to excel; the drinking and harmful types of peer pressure that got him into trouble; poor choices with very little parental guidance or input to help set him on a straighter course. And then there were the PRESCRIPTION PILLS, medication prescribed for a brain (chemical) dysfunction that he could not accept as part of his life.

I see all of these things, and it starts to make some sense. Then I think, "But there are children of negligent parents, single mothers, prostitutes, murderers, child abusers, children with degenerative diseases or missing limbs, and children who may be harmed emotionally by exposure to bad environments—they don't necessarily give up and die by choice."

This rational thinking kept me from falling into an abyss of total guilt and, even worse, continue to blame all of the other participants who played (or should have played) an important role in Weston's life.   I forgave the important characters in his life one by one for their failures, and last, I forgave each of the side-line players: his father, the girl who rejected him, the private school principal, his pastor, his teachers who flunked him, the doctor, etc.

Many months would pass before I began to forgive myself.

August 1987, New Orleans

Last night I joined a club I wish I never had reason to join. The only dues you pay is to survive the self-inflicted death of a loved one. The only meetings you must attend are the ones you muster courage to go to. The only duty of membership is to listen or talk when the need arises.

The organization is called Survivors of Suicide (SOS). Members are not unlike other persons mourning death. Why should they join a group and support one another in their grief? Why do they need to dredge up memories and express the hurting again and again?

Survivors share these things in common: They are desperate to know that someone else understands; others have lived through it; and, they will emerge mentally okay. They share, too, for the most part, the long search for the answer to WHY? The only person who could tell them WHY is gone. The secrets, the pain, the harbored resentments and disappointments in what we, the survivors, did or did not do is buried with them.

We read, study, listen, and watch others who have experienced the same incredulous ordeal in hopes that their story, their suicide notes, their explanations will somehow provide clues to why it happened to us. In other words, "Did my child, my mother, my father, friend, sister, brother, wife, husband choose death over life for a similar reason as another person's loved one?"

It helps to know we all understand each other. Club members almost immediately feel empathy and sorrow for all other members of this hapless group. We allow ourselves to do it. We don't compare tragedies, even though we might not sympathize equally with all the stories:

A fiancee: "I saw it. I watched him do it! He was crazy!"

A wife: "He left me all alone in the new house we'd just built and moved into two months ago."

A husband: "She had tried it before. I thought she was getting better." (He has his new wife of one year there beside him, but he still struggles with grief.)

A mother: "He left two notes saying how much he loved us but just didn't want to live."

A girlfriend: "I'm angry with him. I just want to see him one more time, so I can beat him to a pulp."

An estranged wife: "The police treated me like they
thought I had killed him."

Another wife: "I want to die! I've seen my own death.
I've planned it. I would take pills and just
end it, all this pain!"

A widowed mother: "My child is suffering. He thinks he
will do it, too, just like his father."

An aging couple: "He was our only child. He was thirty-
eight. We will never have another child."

Myself: "I think he was too young to know what it
would be like for someone who found him."

A few of us come, always reluctantly, bitterly, hopefully.
We've not all told our stories. Some just listen. Some never come
back to the club meetings. Some don't come until years after
they are eligible for membership. It doesn't matter to the others.
They don't feel any rejection. The only rejection they are reacting to is the choice of suicide by one they loved and shared life
with—a loss they mourn privately and together.

August 10, 1987 (Sunday)

I cried for my mother again tonight. My mother cannot help
me. She has no power over death or pain that is brought from it.
Still, I cry, "Mama." I turn away from my life and turn inward to
memories, to things that will never be again.

I look to the future and pray that there may be something
there for my daughter, my family, and for me. It is like shuffling
through a deck of cards, knowing that some are missing but that
some playable game may be devised without them.

I'm not sure that I have faced everything as I should, but
daily I am doing the best I can. Each day brings such different
emotions. I am remiss, regretful, weakened, and yet still strug-

gling to survive.

I cry for my mother like a child in pain. The security of having my mother know what to do for me is no longer there. It is amazing how one can live without security, knowing you cannot really trust life.

September 1, 1987

I wrote "Dear Lord, Have Mercy" in a motel room in Chattanooga, Tennessee. Never have I struggled with such anger and indignation at what (I believed) had been done to me. I could not pray; I could not reason; I could not talk to anyone.

This was a terrible night, one of the worst episodes with depression and anger I experienced. The only thing that would help was to write it down and get it out of me. I have asked God's forgiveness and understanding, and I believe that He offers both daily. During this bout with the desire to retaliate, I was led by Him to verses in Ecclesiastes. I am convinced that God had mercy on me and that I was meant to fight this battle with vanity and the vexation of spirit alone that night. He showed me first Ecclesiastes 2:17. And I saw myself therein.

> "Therefore I hated life; because the work that is wrought under the sun is grievous unto me: for all is vanity and vexation of spirit." (Ecclesiastes 2:17)

> " . . . no man can find out the work that God maketh from the beginning to the end." (Ecclesiastes 3:11)

DEAR LORD, HAVE MERCY
(September 1, 1987)

I believe in Him. But I do not find it easy to believe that this is His world. What divine being would create such a cruel, painful, vicious world? What Deity, supremely good and powerful, would wish to be Lord over countless poor, pitiful human beings, searching for meaning and answers for broken lives?

Why would He chance being blamed by them for their misery?

Why would God allow a mother to bear a son, her only son, and create a way for him to die that tortures her for a lifetime? For a lifetime I'll question: Did my son die because I was not a good enough mother or because he innocently inherited a depressive personality due to an incomprehensible malady? Did my son die because I coerced him to take medicines such as Ritalin or because I did not treat his problems soon enough?

Will I ever rid myself of all this torment, these unanswered questions, the unfulfilled life he left behind?

We sing and speak praises to God because He is merciful. But I can't find that mercy in this world. Mercy will come too slowly for me. Healing will come, but I struggle for it. I plead for mercy. When will the bright day come that I have lived long enough to forget like any mother-creature whose young is killed or taken from her through separation? Will I ever forget? No. Not in this life. I would have to live long enough to accept the fact that my boy died alone, that somehow I was neglectful; or, if I had possessed the caring of other mothers, my son would be living still, like theirs. Will I ever live that long?

I cried tonight as if Wes just died yesterday! No one can comfort me. Not God. Not myself.

I can stop crying on the outside. People around me need not see the gaping wound, sense the pain, be met with sad expressions. No open tears are shed for them. No, I can let them live their lives, the lucky ones who will continue to feed and clothe their living children, hold them close and send them off to school. I can and will appear strong. For my living child and for my injured, strife-torn family, I will show an appearance of one who is whole. I love my daughter. I love my family. But I loved him, too.

Inversely, I once imagined if Mary, the mother of Jesus, ever dared to resent God just a little when, in her grief, she would recall her Child's sweetness, His gentleness, and perhaps question why He had to die. She must have known deep sorrow and had many nightmares from the way He was made to suffer, even though, miracle of all miracles, she lived to know that He did rise from the dead, and He was all right! Now, remembering the horror of finding my child dead, I think of her, and I feel a kindred spirit with Mary. Although I am not Catholic, I believe she is the Patron Saint of all mothers who must lose their children in death. She gave birth. She understands.

I lay on a table and brought a child into God's world. He was beautiful and perfect. He was sweet and gentle. He was destined to die by his own hand. For all his pain and anguish over his life as my son saw or perceived it, I did love him and would have him back with me now—not years later in Heaven as we must try to imagine, but now! My mother softly says I will cry when I miss him. But I cry because I am angry, too. Weston did not deserve this. Children who are living today and are not dead as Weston is do not deserve more life, do they? It makes no sense. I am angry. If God did create a world for us to live in, to have children in, then surely it could be a greater monument to Him than it is.

I do not love my life anymore. It has been torn into shreds, and I stumble among the pieces daily. In a Creator's plan, children should not die by suicide. If this were necessary to complete His plan for me, then I wish I had never borne my child, and I wish that I had never been born to know what grief and misery life had in store for me.

I can't live out a "purpose" that may be interpreted for others as a result of my child's tragedy. Will I testify to God's goodness and mercy? Can I? True, my life has been, perhaps, better than some and worse than many. Where do I begin to find the meaning in this in order to show others that I still believe in God's world? Where will I find hope instead of the utter hopelessness I feel? I do not trust life. I do not believe that God "wants me happy," as well-meaning friends have said to me. This leaves me to conclude that if only I were a good person, a better Christian, I could feel that happiness even now.

This moment, the only way that I could feel happiness would be for someone to shake me and say, "Wake up, Kathy. You are crying in your sleep. It is just a dream." Please wake me up from the nightmare that I live with. Please tell me that my son did not kill himself. Please say that he did not feel depression and despair without my knowing it, without my realizing any danger until it was too late to save his life. Tell me he is safe at home and in his room again. Tell me he is happy and looking forward to living. Tell me that there is a tomorrow for him, for us. Please tell me this, and I will love God's world again.

September 20, 1987

THE BIBLE AND MY YOUNG SON'S DEATH

Since opening the Bible that Sunday morning after we lost Wes, I have opened the Bible many times over and found that God doesn't deal in reasons but in sustaining us through our tragedies. Each time I read my Bible, searching for a word of understanding and comfort from Him, I find it without fail.

This is my attempt to put down God's messages to me. I know that many times they were taken out of context—simply a phrase or partial verse—but a few words spoken just to me. I can only say that grief and torture of this magnitude can truly be allayed by God's perfect words and the promise that because of His own sacrifice of a precious Son, I have instant solace that Weston is not gone from me forever. This solace is promised to all Christians. (For if the dead rise not, then is not Christ raised. I Corinthians 15:16)

I testify now that a person cannot comprehend the love that God has for the ones He calls His earthly children until that person has experienced what his own child's death, or other similar tragedy, does to the heart and mind of a body made in His own image. Also, to know that Jesus Christ, God's only Son, was made to suffer and die as His Heavenly Father watched helps us realize that we, as earthly parents, must and can endure.

The first message on that Sunday came when I was very sure in my mind that fear of the memory of finding my child so broken and destroyed would never leave me. It was spoken very

firmly, for it had to be. My tears were pouring down, and my
grief was so severe, I was still nearly screaming in agony. "'God
loves you very much,' he said: 'don't be afraid! Calm yourself;
be strong—yes, strong!' Suddenly, as he spoke these words, I felt
stronger and said to him, 'Now you can go ahead and speak, sir,
for you have strengthened me.'" (Daniel 10:18-19, Living Bible)
But God did not speak. I heard Weston say to me, "I'm all right,
Mom. I see perfect Love, and I've never seen perfect Love before."
My baby, who did not love easily nor receive love readily here
on earth, knew perfect love in Heaven! Later, I related this
experience to my pastor when he came to comfort me. But I had
been comforted.

   The next message was on the Monday, in the early afternoon, before Weston's graveside service. I sat in the rocking chair
next to the window, feeling that my heart was breaking with
grief. I looked down and saw a Psalm that I could not recall or
relocate until weeks later in my own Bible. It spoke of a broken
heart and the promise that God will not leave us to suffer alone.
Part of the verse from Psalm 34:18 is on Weston's monument:
"The Lord is nigh unto them that are of a broken heart . . . " This
is the promise I searched for in the Bible for weeks. He was nigh
unto Wes that night. He is nigh unto us in our mourning and
suffering.

   During the long, slow, torturous weeks following Weston's
death, I alternately blamed myself and others who could not
possibly have known the severity of my son's problems or despair, and I blamed Wes himself for doing this to me and to his
sister. He told us all that he rejected us and our love by dying
of his own volition! The thought of each and every person who
could have done something to stop him and prevent this pain
made me sick with anger. I turned to the Bible for consolation
in this terrible bewilderment and anger. At night I took a Bible
to bed with me, whether my own or a Gideon's Bible I found in a
lonely motel room, just as if it were a warm living being. Skep-
tics call this a religious crutch to help "believers" through times
of crises. Thank you, God, that I am a believer! The Bible was a
friend that could be with me every night. It is still a close,

dependable friend that is always understanding, always promising joy and healing.

When I traveled to Florida, seeking rest and escape early that summer, the Bible was there, opened and waiting, in an unfamiliar family condominium we had rented by the Gulf. A verse from Isaiah, lovingly cross-stitched and framed, hung above it: "When thou passest through the waters, I will be with thee; and through the rivers, they shall not overflow thee; when thou walkest through the fire, thou shalt not be burned; neither shall the flame kindle upon thee." (Isaiah 43:2) How grateful I was to the unsuspecting hostess who must have had a personal reason for making such a beautiful handcrafted picture but whose effort also helped me, a stranger, so greatly in need! I spent that night cradling her Bible to me, thanking God for Isaiah 43:2 and what it meant to me.

Weeks later, in far away Hot Springs, Virginia, I reached into a hotel drawer for the ever-present Bible after recognizing the dangerous feeling that suicide survivors often experience: Why go on? "The Lord did not intervene or give comfort to my loved one!" I screamed silently in my mind. I readily listened to Satan's whisper as I thought, "If He really loved me, He would have, but He turned his back on me," just as Jeremiah had managed to convince himself in the beginning of the third chapter of Lamentations. For whatever reasons, I accused God. He let my child die that way and sentenced me to a life of regrets and suffering. Then I saw, as I read in Lamentations Chapter 3, through my tears that although our souls may be removed "far off from peace" at times, we recall that we have hope (verse 21) and "It is of the Lord's mercies that we are not consumed, because his compassions fail not. They are new every morning; great is thy faithfulness." (Lamentations 3:22-23) "For he doth not afflict willingly nor grieve the children of men." (Lamentations 3:33)

Yes, I have come to know through my bitterness: "The Lord is good unto them that wait for him, to the soul that seeketh him." (Lamentations 3:25) I struggled through books that I did not understand, looking at my faith upside down. Finally, I saw

it all again. As in the months following the death of my beloved younger sister, I continued to pray and try to understand.
It is very hard. The grief comes surprisingly quickly at times,
and it strikes painfully hard. It comes slowly when conjured up
by the heart deliberately or by the mind of the survivor when
he needs to peer back at a memory. The period of mourning will
be there no matter how much comfort the Bible delivers nightly.
But what a lost and deserted feeling, what a dark dismal world
we would look out on each new morning were it not for the Word!
The fulfillment of a promise: We are not alone. Our spirits are
intertwined with our creator. "It is sown a natural body; it is
raised a spiritual body. . . . (I Corinthians 15:44)

Miraculously, and according to our Lord's plan of salvation,
there are words of hope and triumph in the midst of what we
humans consider defeat by death. "The last enemy that shall
be destroyed is death." (I Corinthians 15:26) "And as we have
borne the image of the earthly, we shall also bear the image of
the heavenly." (I Corinthians 15:49)

I feel sorrow for my son and for my life without him. But I
must live it as a testimony to my faith in Him and to my love
for both my Christian children. A greater sorrow is for those
who believe that the Bible and faith are "crutches" for the
religious. To live life well for the sake of living may be noble
enough, but to live life without God and the strength and endless
reserves of love He offers in times of stress and sadness is folly
indeed. Human resources alone, even the most earnest efforts of
our friends and dear loved ones, will at last fail us. We will
question, doubt, and, worst of all, FEAR. The brevity and vanity
of life is a fact. Even the bravest of us are not strong enough to
see ourselves through without Him. "For this God is our God for
ever and ever: He will be our guide even unto death." (Psalms
48:14)

Because I traveled in my work, my pastor had not been
able to be with me or verbalize his feelings about my son's death
or even give me much of his own inner strength and direction for
me to take in my grief. But on a note to me, he wrote "Proverbs
3:5-6." Last night I looked for the passage in the Bible, and I

finally understood. He did realize that a survivor of suicide would torture herself with the many unanswerable WHY'S. He gave me the only heartfelt knowledge he had. This morning (Sunday) while wandering about the house, deciding whether I should go to church or stay to myself against all the reasons built up for not going, I pulled at a very old Bible on the bookshelf, and the cover came away in my hand. Written at the very top, in my grandmother's handwriting, was, "Remember Proverbs 3:5-6." Those two verses are: "Trust in the Lord with all thine heart; and lean not unto thine own understanding. In all thy ways acknowledge him, and he shall direct thy paths."

Allowing myself a good long cry once again, I dressed and drove to church.

September 20, 1987

EXCERPTS FROM LETTER TO MY PASTOR

I wanted to share these things with you because I knew you were troubled over Weston. I see clearly that you are very fond of the youth in our church. Your greatest tolerance and compassion lie with them, and you are demonstrative in your affection for them. I have not been there to see, but I have wondered how much was done to help them understand their feelings about the suicidal death of a friend. We know so little about suicide in our small town. Not one single person came forth to tell me what to read or how to seek help, but, fortunately, I did it on my own. Through my search for my own help, I have learned that **many** of our children may still be needing help, but not finding any. Silence on the subject seems to be the way we respond to their confusion and pain.

There are many books that are excellent on this subject and should be on our library shelves. There should also be suggested reading for persons who have experienced sudden death, violence, and grief. The Bible is and has been my strengthening force against giving way to despair, but there has also been some very much needed reading done in other places to help me understand my horrible guilt, anger, depression, and own suicidal feelings over my son's death.

Did you know I went through a period of severe anger? It included an anger toward God which frightened me. I was angry at you, too. . . . I'll never forget your coming to talk to him [about joining the church] and then telling me he was not "ready." I was afraid Wes would be lost. But when he was twelve, he prayed to receive Jesus in his heart on a church youth trip . . .

That day, in answer to my prayers, he went to the church and professed his faith. I believe the Lord knew how difficult it was for Wes to express himself. I am enclosing a story that I wrote about him when he was ten years old. I wanted you to know something about Weston's short life. It is not an explanation for his death, but it helps to know some things. Nothing but dying was ever going to be easy for Weston. It is over for him now, but so many children go on hiding this pain from their parents and peers, putting a brave face forward, but inside they are full of fear and confusion. If you have not talked to the children about death, it is time to do so now. I felt before that to mention the act would put "ideas into their heads." People who are studying the teenage suicide epidemic in our country tell us that they are there already. Talking and getting them to talk is our only hope of fighting this enemy. Wes did tell his friends that he wanted to die. Have our teenagers been alerted that they should listen for signals like this and seek help? Is it because we are a small community that we are to hope that Weston and the child that committed suicide soon after Weston did were isolated incidents, and the suicide "angel of death" has passed over and taken what would be taken?

I have decided that I must help other people who have been through this, and although they know the Lord, they will still need so much help. I am praying for God to open up ways for me to bring that help to others. Please pray for me, too. I was counseled by a Christian lady who advised me to talk to you. Well, I am not brave enough for much talking now. I do feel better for the writing and hope that you will understand.

Love,
Kathy

October 31, 1987 (Halloween)

On Halloween night I was getting ready for the trick-or-treaters that would come, I knew, even though the entire town was aware that Weston had killed himself in this house. I imagined how the youngsters might be caught up in the idea that Weston's spirit may still linger in some way in his bedroom on the far front of the house. I wished that the whole world would go away. Every minute of the night was filled with real haunting memories for me. Why did I remain here? I could not leave; I had to face all these emotions now. I had to get used to holidays without him.

Finally, I gave in to the relentless memories that assailed my broken heart, declared a truce with my self-tormenting, got a pen and paper and began to write:

October 31, 1987

Hi Weston,

It is the first Halloween without you and Shea at home. I have missed you both so much today. I went outside to see the leaves falling, and that made me feel better. Don't think I have ever cried so much to have you and Shea back home as I have the last few days. I miss you both so much.

Weston, in your death I see a finality of things we will never do or look forward to again. Shea's away at college now and because home will never be quite "home" again to her with you gone, things are so very sad. I am a lonely, lonely mother. Your mother is filled with regrets that she didn't appreciate enough the times the three of us were together. But, Baby, I was so tired, and it seemed, so burdened. How light the tiny burdens of former days seem now!

Remember how you hated the old woman's mask I would put on every Halloween night to greet the Trick-or-Treaters? How we laughed! I can still open the door to the children, but I don't need that old mask to look pitiful.

On your first Halloween hunt around the neighborhood with your big sister, you carried a little pumpkin. You didn't know the custom very well, so every time a door would open, you tried to go inside. I had to lean down and hold you back, and Shea would help me stop you from sitting down to eat your candy between houses.

These holidays are for children. You were my children, you and Shea. I can't have you back little again or any other way, now. I want our times together back again.

Just wanted you to know.

Love,
Mom

December 24, 1987

CHRISTMAS ANGELS

My red-headed boy is an angel now
Though on earth we could seldom see
Angelic qualities nor lofty demeanor,
But he was as sweet as he knew how to be.

I'm missing him so at Christmastime,
I'm wondering how he fares
Without his Mom and big sister
And his youthful earthly cares.

Do they make snow ice cream in heaven?
Does he miss the "forests" or trees?
Or lazing close to a nice, warm fire
With a Christmas story to read?

Do they have rock music in heaven
For the younger souls to hear?
He was never much of a "Choir Boy,"
But music to him was dear.

Does he sing now with Christmas Angels
With a heart filled with timeless joy?
Is Jesus' birthday a celebration still
That thrills and excites my boy?

What if they don't have chocolate?
He would miss that more than the rest!
He loved "M & Ms," especially,
And chocolate chip cookies best.

I guess there's no need to decorate
A home as beautiful as his,
But I think he'd like trimming the tree
With ornaments reserved for Wes.

And if there are puppies or baby rabbits
That he might be allowed to hold,
This would be a special heavenly gift,
For to him it would never grow old.

When I see Christmas Angels,
I really can't help but pray
That he still has all his boyish charm
I miss so much everyday.

And that he's a diligent young angel
Complete with adoration
For the Christ who made a home for him
And has given me consolation.

                                        Kathleen Sandefer

CHAPTER 16

I continued on into and through 1988 reading everything I could find to console my broken heart or to try to understand about teenage suicide—anything to keep from hurting so much for just a little while.

I continued to write to try to express my feelings, to analyze and reconcile myself to Wes' death.

February 1988

Weston's personality, his school work, and his life were affected by a rarely recognized condition called Minimal Brain Dysfunction [now referred to as Attention Deficit Disorder], diagnosed by the doctor when he was ten years old. I learned that one out of six children (over 80% boys) are born with this genetic defect. In adolescence, his gradual realization of how different he was because of the required daily medication and limited control over his thought processes, as well as his limited motor coordination, overwhelmed him and depressed him. It may have even made him believe that he was rejected by various people because of the "affliction." He had to have known that this must be why learning to drive would not come easily, nor would skiing, tennis, basketball, or football. I guess he felt this must be why he was so dependent on his mother and sister.

As the realization sank in, he rebelled against what he did not understand or want to accept. His refusal to take the medicine compounded his problems in school. The drinking that his young friends thought was fun to do caused him to spiral out of control.

I have thought so many times that I was too protective and

indulgent. I have wondered how else I could have helped him. Counseling may have been beneficial, but his fervent desire for privacy would have made this an uphill struggle. Just to suggest it may possibly have been more of a crushing blow.

What might have helped a youth caught in the abrupt changes of puberty while having to adjust, too, to the fact that his brain would not function properly without medication? Special tutors? Intensive monitoring of his youthful activities? A more stable home environment? More time with his father? Which, if any, of these factors might have corrected the susceptibility to depression?

In my self-flagellation immediately after the suicide, I wondered if not allowing him to keep the gun in his room would have postponed or eliminated the dangerous preoccupation with suicide. As a survivor of suicide, I must find some peace in believing that he did not want to live if he had to suffer and that he made the decision with which he was satisfied. But, contrarily, Weston did not appear depressed that last Saturday of his life. He had a very normal day, eating, laughing, playing.

Yet, late that night they tore the ruined ceiling tiles and bedroom carpet out and took his things away. When I got Weston's clothes, pillows, and bedspreads back from the cleaners, I could still hear him saying that same Saturday afternoon that his closet was too full. He asked to clean out old clothes to make room for his new things. Why, Wes? What changed your mind about living another day that particular night?

People try to help you, the survivor. They grope for the right thing to say: "God saw Wes was getting into trouble. He took him home before anything worse could happen later." Anything WORSE? What could be worse?

"We don't know what happens with the suicide victim, Kathy. Their minds just snap, and in that split second . . . He did not stop to think. If he had, he wouldn't have done it."

"It's God's will, Kathy. He has a plan for you, and you are going to need to pray and ask Him to show you what it is. Maybe you are going to help others because of your misfortune."

The God I love and worship "planned" for me to see my

son's brains spilled out on the floor? I will never see Wes again just so I might be able to understand the grief and pain of others and be locked into some type of service?

I would nod my head and say that I understood, but this one line from Robert L. Veninga's "A Gift of Hope" finally explained the mystery of what happened, when it happened, best for me: "You must agree that suicide for your loved one was the only path that he could have taken."

Veninga continued, "Your recovery will only begin when you give unconditional pardon. Forgive the victim; forgive the poor helpless survivors as well. It will end when you sense that your loved one is better off in death than in life."

Pardon the one who is gone and, as Marjorie Holmes wisely advised in her book, *To Help You Through the Hurting*, "Let him go!" In the book, *When Bad Things Happen to Good People* by Harold S. Kushner, we are told that we are not singled out for grief by a God who "plans" purposeful tragedy. We are simply sometimes among the unlucky and unfortunate. "Do not put God's finger on the trigger," he urged.

I don't. But neither do I spend anymore futile moments in prayers that begin: "Oh, Lord, please watch over . . . " or "God, please don't let . . ." or "Thank you, Lord, for keeping us safe and healthy." I felt a sudden estrangement from the God I thought I knew and understood. I believed after Jan's death and my son's suicide that He was powerless to intervene on our behalf and watch over us with some invisible protective umbrella.

When Jan was dying of cancer in 1983, I went to the hospital chapel believing that with fervent prayer from a true believer, the course of the disease could be altered by God. I felt a sense of warmth and well-being after I prayed that afternoon. I felt His presence. And so, misinterpreting my feelings of comfort from this time of prayer as being an affirmative answer, I felt betrayed when her condition declined rapidly, and the doctors never gave us any word of hope. In fact, it became so apparent that she would only continue to suffer from this terminal illness that relatives and friends began to pray for an end to it all.

My mother, who always stalwartly loved and worshiped

God, had raised the four of us children in the church. She became hurt, bitter, untrusting, and confused after the ordeal, but she went on believing and wondering why she was punished. We were impatient with her to heal as fast as we children did. Now I understand her anguish. She emerged gracefully and even more loving and kind. She was a role model for me. Of course, our minds are clouded by grief, and we think about our Creator as little children do, making the confusion about what happens to us even greater.

My own catharsis was abetted by years of praying in my Sunday School Class with a group of young women who attempted to gain God's miraculous involvement in anything from a whiplash in a husband's neck to a baby girl undergoing torturous treatment for leukemia to save her life. When prayers were answered in a positive way, we never discussed the fact that some prayers, like those for my sister, were not.

Although there may be a purpose in my life developing due to Weston's death, I can say that God did not then give me any indication of it. "Perhaps I should attempt to tell all," I would say to myself. Maybe my purpose was to try to communicate with other unsuspecting parents of MBD [or ADD] children who will no doubt reach this stage in their already terribly disrupted maturation and development. But my few attempts toward this end were rejected. The doctor told me that concerning these children, warnings about suicide from effects of the medication would not be a healthy thing.

Should Weston's life be given up and nothing positive come out of his having lived on this earth? But Wes, my son, never wanted anyone to know! I can still hear him crying out like the little boy I lived with and knew so well, "Don't tell! Don't tell!" I can hear him say, "Mom, I can do it without the medicine. You have to believe me! Mom, I'm all right."

Therein lies the stifling incongruity in finding a purpose. I would like for all newspapers to carry the entire story, but would anyone care once it was spilled out? Would it convince anyone that they could help MBD [or ADD] children get through their lives any easier? Would Weston want to be labeled and have complete strangers know of his problems facing life? Would his surviving sister? His grandparents? If it requires baring our souls to the world or at least to people who cared enough to read my story, is it a worthy purpose? And is it God's will?

I say forget trying to tell anyone in mourning that the brain of the suicide victim just "snapped." Forget advising the survivor to accept it as God's will and that He had a purpose unless you are sure you are immune to tragedy. Some people actually think, "It didn't happen in our family because we are doing the **right** things with our children." Then, as if to prove themselves correct, look for evidence of this and say, "Why, look how happy and well-adjusted they are." Some parents, like I did, take their children's desire for self-preservation for granted. God forbid that they should ever suffer what bereaved parents suffer for any reason—accident, illness, suicide.

I want to scream in people's faces, "Please listen!" I want to shout at them, "Wes wasn't so different that this should have happened!" I want to tell them that he is not even an isolated case. Can't they see? If one child like him feels such agony that he must kill himself, where will we begin to stop the future self-destruction of others, even now being judged "special" by our school systems. Maybe not self-destruction by suicide but by violent rebellion against the unfairness of it all, rebellion against society because of the need to be "accepted." The desire to succeed and be counted among the fortunate few, such as the top students in school, the athletic heroes, the popular ones, are not woes of only the MBD child, but MBD [or ADD] children are the ones who must live with the labels. They are always striving silently to accept being the ones who don't make the grade, being relegated to the LD (Learning Disabled) and the slow-learner classes. They live in a frustrating world of structured classroom environments with teachers who do not want to be bothered with the "hyper," "attention deficient," or "troublesome" child. These children feel different. Many must feel hopeless.

Professional counseling and medication cannot always be the definitive answer for these children. Besides, it is rare anyway. The cost is prohibitive, the social stigma too fearsome, the effort too demanding.

If we are to alter the results of rejection, failure, and misunderstanding of MBD [or ADD] children, we must work for a public awareness of the problem beyond a few trained and semi-trained special education teachers, a spattering of experiments with mainstreaming, and tired words from psychologists. We must learn more about treatment that is available.

I want to respect my son's wish for privacy, but I also want to warn others who possibly must face personal tragedy by seeing their children imprisoned, committed to mental institutions, or commit suicide.

Do children who are viewed with contempt in our school systems accept with grace that they are what they are because they are learning disabled (LD), hyperkinetic, MBD [or ADD], or any other branding categories other than "normal"? When they are placed on medication with no counseling and expected to take drugs (in a society that considers drugs a bad thing) without knowing why, do they understand? Would adults?

I know that someone else will have to deal with this. I have written pages and pages about what I believe to be the reason or reasons for my son's death. Sometimes, I can only feel that this is all in vain. It won't bring Weston back. But if it will save one child from choosing death for the same reasons or prevent just one mother from going through the grief I live with, my efforts will have served its purpose.

February 14, 1988

A VALENTINE FOR WESTON

I don't wish to sing a song of tears,
Only bring back a memory of happy years.
Though it sometimes breaks my heart in two,
I have to say I still think of you.

A silent song is sung for my boy,
A yearning theme of remembered joy.
It is almost as if your voice I can hear
On the strains of love that bring you near.

Now that we have come to the end of our days,
May you know that I've missed you in so many ways.
I'll never forget how you once played here
Before the sorrow, before the tears.

A melody of remembrance that hums in my ears
After the sorrow, after the tears.

                                        Kathleen Sandefer

Spring 1988

SQUARING OFF AT ANGER

YOU have been injured. You feel undeserved pain in the
very core of your being. Your injury is intensified by the knowledge that your loved one must have been also injured. It is not
enough to blame yourself; you will find accomplices. People will
surface who had a little or a lot to do with your loved one's life
and perhaps his unhappiness—a boss, a girlfriend, a school
principal, peers, and others.

You will also resent the lack of intervention from innocent
people whose influence you counted on, such as a pastor, teachers, step-parents, grandparents, estranged mates. You will
harbor this dark resentment, and finally it will turn into hard
anger. Ultimately, you may even turn your anger on God. You
may feel that nothing else matters except "getting it out." Some
authors who write about dealing with anger after a suicide
state: You may turn your anger on God. He can handle it. Don't
confront others with anger. It will hurt and confuse them, and
then you will heap more guilt on yourself.

But can you risk blaming God for letting the suicide happen? Do you need to handle that isolation, too? Anger and isolation toward God is a one way street headed for a dead end. Cry out to Him in anguish, remand your loved one to His care, ask His mercy and grace to sustain you, but don't try to blame Him. His world is imperfect because of human pitfalls, but His Word promises a different ending for it all.

Confess your anger and discuss any blame you feel toward yourself, your family, or any others with a close friend or counselor. If you don't really want to express the anger aloud, write about it and then let it go. It is not all right to be angry at God. You will need God, your Father, now more than you did in better days before the tragedy. Let Him listen to you and care for you. It is His promise that all tears will be wiped away.

May 2, 1988

This is the day, May 2. I had planned to go over every small detail of May 2 last year, remember it all one last time, give it a good wringing out, wail, gnash my teeth, spill my guts, do a lot of crying. I had planned to burn a candle by his picture, something I imagined one can do for their dead. I planned to visit the cemetery, taking some special remembrance from his room, something peculiarly him. God knows there were enough things he left behind to choose from. I didn't do any of these things, and now, I'm sure I won't.

What I was doing, finally, by 7:45 p.m. was writing. I had to tell his story. Weston had to have known he faced not only humiliating taunts at school that next week, the consequences of failing, but also not being able to pass the driver's test. What a nightmare his life had become for him. Even if he had told me about his pain, what could I have done?

He's gone now, and I look out through the same windows, at the same flowers I gazed on last spring when he was alive. Last spring, when the next day, he was dead. There is a kind of inner peace of acceptance, intermixed with tears that start suddenly for no reason now except that I miss him. Most of his things are gone or given away. A very few things were returned

to his room. His telescope stands untouched. His books and
the school bag bearing his name remain packed as if ready to
go back to school when the impossible should happen: He would
return. His sixteenth birthday would be this summer.

May 2, 1988

SOMETHING FOR YOU, WES

I want to do something for you, Wes.
I want to tell who you were.
You were my son, though you ended your life,
Your mother's grief and her love will endure.

I remember you every morning, Wes,
In the quietness before we would stir.
I imagine you could still be asleep in your room,
The beautiful boy that you were.

I go to the kitchen to make coffee,
Open the cabinet only to see
The cups and the bowls and recall so well
That the first thing you did was to eat!

The meals that you liked for breakfast
There's no need to make anymore,
No pancakes, cereal or hot chocolate,
No cinnamon toast as before.

I remember the pills in the later years
That you took daily as if they were needed.
With a mixture of sorrow and pity for us both,
I almost wish we had never heeded
The advice of the doctor, but let you be YOU,

So at least I could have been sure
That the boy who was sad and ended his life
Was really the boy that you were.

I look out at the yard in the light of day
As the breeze stirs the leaves across the lawn.
I imagine you could be out of sight and at play
Happy once more, safe from harm.

I can see your auburn hair and tanned smooth skin
On your youthful and lanky frame.
I think you might answer from somewhere out there
If only I would call your name.

I want to do something for you, Wes,
So to the lonely cemetery I go.
There's no solace there, no change, no life,
The silk flowers don't even grow.

Along with our little dog I circle your grave,
There's nothing I can do but gaze
At the cross that stands as a monument
To the years of the life that you gave.

I want to do something for you, Wes,
Your memory always to keep,
But as the months and years slip by, I find
That all I can do is weep.

I return home alone and live helplessly
With the knowledge that this will never change,
This wanting to do something for you, Wes,
Other than silently suffering the pain.

So often I sit and remember
And look at your picture and things.
I write long poems such as this one
For just me to read.

Then to bed I go
And sometimes, you know?
You live. You live once again
In my dreams.

                              Kathleen Sandefer

May 4, 1988 (Anniversary of the Funeral)

AND YOU MOURN

The night bird twills a few soft notes
The moment 'tween midnight and morn
Your eyes are clouded with tears again,
Your heart is heavy and torn.

Grief comes stalking in waves of pain
And you mourn,
And you mourn,
And you mourn.

You search for signs of the life now gone
A keepsake, a photo forlorn,
Did you give birth to a life or a death?
Where is the child so warm?

Can you recapture a moment in time
With a laughing baby in your arms entwined?
You danced 'round and 'round, never doubting
That the child would forever be healthy and fine.

Can you remember the happier days
Of childhoods left behind, both Weston's and Shea's,
Without remembering the loss you've endured
That too soon the innocence became obscured?

Bright eyes that twinkled with joy in life
You remember dulled with mysterious strife.
You may never hold him or touch him again,
Kiss him goodnight or care for him.

The hapless person you've become, you scorn,
And you mourn,
And you mourn,
And you mourn.

                              Kathleen Sandefer

June 1988

I hear the mourning for my child in the whispering pines
near the house we lived in, in the call of the doves that have
returned for the summer, in the sounds of teenage songs that
tell the sad stories of their tumultuous states of heart. Sometimes I can feel thankful that he was spared anymore certain
pain, and I can relive sweet memories instead of the more painful ones that the suicide had left me in earlier months.

Probably the most difficult part of accepting Weston's
death is knowing how beautiful he was, how strong and handsome he had become. Yet, life was still strange and alien to him.
How much Wes had to offer had he only opened up and let himself live with his limitations. I cannot stand the thought of his
believing that death was the best course for him. I cannot bear
knowing that he felt that way about himself, if only for a few
moments before he lifted the gun to his head. I loved him and
told him so every day. Why couldn't he love himself more than
that? What could I have done for my child to alter his personality or his final act of vengeance upon himself? How could he

have known in his child's mind that he would leave us all so
stunned and forever remorseful?

Why do some children survive the desire to self-destruct
and others carry it out? Where does this kind of desperate courage to bring about what is unnatural to every living thing come
from? Do they regret the action even during the irreversible
pressure on the trigger, the snap of the rope, the drooping of
the eyes as the pills or gas take effect? Are they really aware
that what they do will mean everlasting finality, will inject
sadness into the lives of loved ones left behind? Do they wish
it? Do they care? Did they know or refuse to care how loved
they were?

These are not all unanswered questions, but the answers
do not satisfy. So we go on, those seeking to know the answers,
and find instead acceptance and healing.

June 18, 1988

I understand the death wish. People say, "I can't understand how anyone could do something like that." That puzzling
enigma is the act of suicide, but I can understand it now.

Not two weeks after the death of Weston, I had sunk rapidly into an abyss of pain and depression. There were so many
times that I wanted desperately to follow him, find him in death
before it was too late. After all, the poor human spirit knows
nothing of the death traveler and how far the journey will take
our deceased loved ones. This death wish, I read, was natural
and experienced by others. But life goes on, and the ties to remain here with the other mourners, to be comforted and strengthened by them, and to ultimately come out of this state keeps us
here.

This morning, June 18, 1988, I came as close to taking my
own life as I did last New Year's Eve morning when I struggled with it and cried until I was sick, choking and coughing,
finally falling into an exhausted sleep. I contemplated death
not to find Wes but to escape this world. This crucial difference
helped me understand his act. As much as I love him and my

daughter, Shea, who still lives and holds the promise of future joys for me, the pain of living just another day was so overshadowing that it hid every hope, every human tie, and every shred of far reaching compassion for the family members who would have to cope once more with the death and loss of a loved one.

There is a menacing voice in the brain of one who feels this way. I could hear myself saying: "I'll never go back to church again. God doesn't love me. I have a pain in my breast, and I know I am going to die. He plans to let me die like my sister, Jan." Even now I start to cry as I write these words: "God is punishing me; I know it. My whole life has been a punishment. I am not allowed to be happy, not meant to be happy ever again or to know any peace."

Now, I have really begun to fall down the tunnel of self-pity and depression, at the end of which there is no light. I am naked without defense against the attacks on my tenuous grasp on what new life I am trying to rebuild. These are examples: I am alone now and not by choice. Shea has gone to live this summer with her daddy and step-mother. I believe they are trying to take my place in her college decisions. I have no one who understands me. I am only meant to make money and be there to hold the pieces together in case someone needs me. Mostly for money. That is the only thing I can do.

Then my tortured mind reaches for something to defend itself with. It senses real danger now and rightly so, because the crying is out of control and the pain in my stomach is leaving my mind vulnerable to self-destructive thoughts.

Now I have left the kitchen where I was having my morning coffee, seeking the close private sanctity of my bedroom where I can try to think. Crying still harder, my mind brings up the recollection of the man in my life. He doesn't really want me either, I say. I am such an emotional cripple, who would want me? Besides, there is no life left to be lived. My children are gone, and there is no one left to be there for. I can't start over; I can't be young again. Others have that, but not me. I can only work and make money, and how do I know I can do that very much longer?

My mind says, "But remember Shea, Mother and Daddy, and my brother and sister. Don't take the pills and let them find you dead, not knowing if they had been there sooner or seen the signs, they could have stopped you." But I think the sickest response of all, and one that shows the suicide victim's viewpoint on life at the time of the act, is: THEY WILL BE BETTER OFF WITHOUT ME. I AM ONLY A BURDEN! **AND EVERYBODY IS GOING TO DIE ANYWAY**. THAT IS WHAT LIFE IS, DYING, AND I DON'T WANT TO BE HERE TO SUFFER ANYMORE.

One might call this really "warped," but in the state of depression that I was in for that span of time, there were no bright thoughts about my having grandchildren. There were no intelligent ideas about how I could make life meaningful for others, forgetting my own loss and being helpful to those even less fortunate in some way. Last, there were no hopeful signs that this depression, or the factors that continue to bring it back, would ever go away. AND I KNEW I DID NOT WANT TO LIVE WITH THAT KIND OF REALITY!

Wes, my son, had killed himself. I thought that my daughter sought the happy "normal" life her father now could provide for the remainder of her dependent years. I was a failure and a walking shell of a human being. I did not even want to be with me. Lined up among my enemies were people I loved or once loved. Nobody understood or wanted to know about my grief. None of these people could sustain my life or MAKE ME WANT TO LIVE. I had to do this for myself.

With my head down and still crying, I thought of lining up all the pills I could find there in the bathroom drawers and cabinets. There had to be enough, but was there enough time? I could take the pills to deaden the pain and then slash my wrists. Surely, there would be no turning back then.

I lifted my head up and looked into the face of my son in the black and white picture in a blue frame I kept there on the dresser top. I said, "Now I understand what brought you that far—a hard and ugly feeling of self-doubt, worthlessness, and misery." How could a child of his age deal with such pain? Why would he want to try?

I recognized what was happening to me for what it was—a bout of depression so severe that it threatened to destroy me, like a severe case of flu can kill the already weakened body of an elderly person. I was weakened by the death of my child and loneliness of the early summer days when, in fact, no one that knew me could fathom the very deep dismal feelings I was enduring because I hid them, even from my closest relatives.

If I had committed suicide, I mused, everyone would have said, "But I thought she was doing so well." I wondered if anyone would have said, "I can understand how she would do something like that."

I got up and dressed, the cleansing tears subsiding, and walked outside into the hot dry air of summer. The first thing I saw on the ground just six feet from the door was a baby martin. I looked up to the martin house nearby to see if the mother was chirping or upset. But all were gone. Gone about the business of life, I supposed. And the baby martin would no longer be part of their living except for having been in the nest with its mother and having been cared for and nurtured awhile. Its life was shortened for some unexplained reason while the other nestlings flew away to perpetuate life in the scheme of nature. No one could ever say why that particular one could not continue to live.

An absurd thought occurred to me. Did the little martin's mother live less happily now because of the loss of that life she brought into the world? Did she feel depression as I did? If not, how lucky the birds were that they could fly away and begin anew each season without the painful memories that we humans must tolerate. How lucky that they must never experience the death wish.

August 1988

THE OFFENSE OF SELF-DEFENSE

Loneliness and depression are natural enemies of the mourner. The two dark invaders lurk in one's mind when recovering from loss. If you like to be with people, try not to keep yourself away from others when under attack. "Aloneness" can bring on depression and heighten it.

You probably will find the conversations you must tolerate to be with people will awaken so many memories that it will be quite difficult to follow talk of children, husbands, or other commonplace topics without bringing up your own experiences. You yearn to remind these people that not so long ago, "I was just like you"; however, you think you must keep silent. Avoid thinking that way. Mentioning a loved one who recently died may present an aftershock to the listener, but your need to talk about your loss is pressing. You think, "I'm into the conversation now with my own memories to present to you." This is a kind of offense, not meant to be hostile, not seeking sympathy, but more to say, "Listen. Am I to sustain your enjoyment of having me be an audience to your children's current problems, activities, achievements, or your concerns about them and not let you know that I am still there, too, in limbo, hovering between recent life and current death? My child may be gone to you but not my child's life's impressions on me. There can be no future to speak of, but there definitely was a lifetime to remember, however short." **This is the offense of self-defense**. Should you make others uncomfortable watching your animated face and listening to your recounting memories of a dead child? Should you allow them to feel intimidated by your loss by having your child seem as if he or she still "belongs" in the conversation of the living?

I went to church one Sunday after losing Wes. I had finally reconciled myself to having to glance at the restless teenagers whose lives my son once touched so closely. They always sat in the front and center pews of the church. How many Sundays had I searched out his easily spotted red head of hair? But no longer, even though I can still see the backs of his friends' heads, the youthful haircuts like his, the strong shoulders beginning to fill out plaid shirts like his. They lean forward on elbows like he always did. I could control myself enough to hold back tears, knowing he would never sit there with them again. Then we stood to sing songs. First, "When the Roll is Called Up Yonder." No sounds from my voice would come. Then next, "When We All Get to Heaven." I thought angrily, "Did they save all of the songs about the glory of dying for me this Sunday morning?" I felt assaulted and sorry for myself.

Depression was suddenly taking its hold after several days of being okay. I was sinking and knew very well that the Sunday visit to the cemetery would be a tearful one that day. The tears did come and brought a relief from the sorrow, temporarily, I knew, but any relief was met with gratitude.

That afternoon, I attended a party at which young mothers enthusiastically discussed school and their children. I tried to speak of my own children, including Weston, because I needed to feel alive and unseparated from life as I once lived it. In doing so, I opened up a store of memories and had a really good talk with another mother. It was a self-defense against depression. I was continuing the battle.

I had taken the risk of causing discomfort or intimidation, seemingly selfishly, but it resulted in her telling me candidly about the suicide attempt of her sister's sixteen-year-old son. She shared with me her anguish for her sister and her nephew. She sought advice. I told her that I had not become an expert on suicide prevention, but I knew some things I wish I had done if I had only had the chance.

Communication is an offense of self-defense. It helps us hold our own against depression until the next day, which may be better. Sometimes, though, you just may not be able to face others. That will be all right, too, if you can find a way to release your feelings, writing, talking to yourself, reminding yourself that you are not perfect. You are only a human with mourning to do because you still love and miss your child.

August 1988

SOOTHING THE SORROWS OF THE WORLD

I never liked to read newspapers. They are filled with articles of horrible atrocities man can deliver his fellowman. In particular, I dread reading of deliberate or negligent acts that cause children to suffer. I remember being so affected by continuous stories of child abuse that I carried a burden on my heart, crying for all of them and praying at length to God to intervene and prevent the suffering of children at the hands of their parents to whom they look for love and protection.

I had read only a month before Wes' suicide about the suicide pact of four teenagers who, together, climbed into a car and ended their lives by asphyxiation. I remember being thankful that my two children, albeit experiencing most typical teenage setbacks while making the problem-beset uphill climb toward maturity, were at least secure, loved, and safe from danger or abuse. My impression was that the three of us had a "handle" on life, and those poor families must have left out something terribly important. I discounted suicide as an act my children were capable of or that either of them would ever resort to as a way out. Besides, their lives were too normal.

I was unaware, of course, that within my own walls, my son and daughter had consoled each other and confessed that they had thoughts of killing themselves because life was hard sometimes. In the high school annual that spring, my son was writing suicidal messages to his friends, such as "Take care of yourself. I won't be around anymore to help you out," etc.

Because of this ignorance of my child's depression that led to his death wish, I have been thrust into a new awareness of hurting, real or potential, on the part of other children. Any type of suffering or need that I imagine I might alleviate, even temporarily, evokes empathy in me. I "adopted" a small boy through the Christian Children's fund. I give money to lone children longingly eyeing candy displays, smiles and kind words to children with sorrowful looks, offerings to children's charities, and unsolicited advice to parents expressing frustration with their offspring.

I have also imagined myself adopting unwanted children, joyfully, to give myself a purpose (or do penance), being a foster parent, or even opening a home for troubled youths. This feeling of guilt that must be attended to by sacrifice on my part is one of the most difficult emotions with which I have had to deal. I see thousands of people, wealthier and more capable than I, never going out of their way to soothe the sorrows of the world. To feel responsibility for the world's injustices may be natural for a suicide survivor, but it can be overwhelming and obsessive. Hence, you find many, many counselors who have themselves experienced the horror of their children's suicides.

This need will begin to slacken as grieving begins to diminish, and most of us will feel we even deserve a happy life again. A person whose child committed suicide may resume a life without guilt, without pondering the sorrow all about, without feeling a rush of sympathy or indignation for any hurting child. The grieving diminishes for me when I feel I have done some little something to better the world. Is it bad for any of us to be more aware that wrong things happen because we are unseeing, unhearing, uncaring, or uneducated? No, but don't try to carry all the blame or debt to society in your heart because of this terrible thing that has happened to you.

Before my son's suicide, I prayed fervently something could be done to save the world from the atrocities that are inevitably a part of it. Helpless as I am, I console myself by thinking I must be a good person for having prayed about it. I like to think that it makes me a caring person rather than an apathetic one who does not care at all. And so, as the cliche says, "Life goes on."

It is your life which must go on. You and I must forgive ourselves for the sake of ourselves and others about us who love us and whom we love. We can find as our guilt subsides that we don't owe a debt to society for the death of a person we loved, and we don't have to prove our worth to the world.

January 3, 1989

Facing a new year is still difficult for me. I recognize that healing has occurred though, because the intense grief over incidental happenings and holidays has begun to lessen. I find that I can go for several days at a time without the need to huddle into myself and deal with the loss of Wes, but not a day goes by that I do not think of him, mourn for him, or miss him.

Suffering the loneliness of loss evokes a dual impact of self-pity and self-deprecation. I find that now I frequently feel alone and deserted. I want to seek God's help, to take courage that the emotional quality of life for me will improve, but sometimes I feel hopeless. I want to be happy again, feel safe again. I want to stop being self-absorbed; nevertheless, I must learn to live with myself and be patient with my own needs. On January 1, 1989, I wrote:

> I don't want the New Year to begin! It is 1989 already! That much more time has passed which will erase the memory of Weston's short existence on this earth. As I write this, I know my heart is broken by many things. I have never really gotten past my divorce and how much it affected my life and my children's lives. I have barely gotten over the death of my sister and now will face the suicide of my son for the rest of my life.

> To lose Jan and to lose Weston creates a double void in my life. I needed them, for their lives sustained both the dependent and the nurturing sides of me. Why did they have to be taken away? And why so cruelly? No longer do I have Weston to take care of or Jan to reassure me. Death has claimed them both. I feel such despair tonight that I want to go with them in death, too. What keeps me from it? The hope that, somehow, "joy will come in the morning."

January 1, 1988, had been such an arduous morning. I believed then that Weston's death would make me suffer nightly, wondering why and where did I fail, and for this reason I could not face a new year. Shea had left early to drive back to south Louisiana to spend the last of the holidays with her father's family, and I felt the extreme loneliness. Finally, I turned to the Bible to search for some kind of peace. I read Proverbs 3:24: "When thou liest down thou shalt not be afraid: yea, thou shalt lie down, and thy sleep shall be sweet." After reading this verse, I found that each night became a little easier to get into bed, think about Shea and her future or what I might do with the rest of my life, then fall off to sleep.

Beyond my own reassurance I pray that the words God showed me and which I have made reference to here might be helpful to some lonely being. I know I am not the only mother, sister, or divorced woman in the world to know multiple sorrows. In verse 27 of Proverbs 3, the Lord told me, "Withhold not good from them to whom it is due, when it is in thine hand to do it." I asked the Lord what good could come from my revealing such struggles with sadness and suffering. Repeatedly, I asked Him what good could come from disclosing the private details of my son's brief life and tragic death. I heard Him say, "Trust me."

March 1989

I had watched my sister die. Week after week, month after month, she died slowly. Once, near the end, she sat up in bed, disoriented from the drugs she was taking for pain and said to me, "Let's put on our shorts and go out to the ball park to watch the children." I looked at her and said, "We can't do that today, Jan." We held each other in an embrace of defeat on the side of her hospital bed. She, wanting to give up the battle but desperate to live for her family, and I, wanting to encourage her to go on fighting but praying that she would be relieved of the suffering. Driving home late that night alone in my car, I began to scream, trying to release the pent up frustrations and fear that mounted day after day that were repressed while I was near her. I couldn't face giving her up.

After Jan's death, I returned to everyday duties, resolved

to get on with life because my children needed me. I looked
forward to spending more time with them again, to fulfill
the purpose I felt God meant for me, to be a good mother, to make
a home for the children, to give them support. Jan's courage in
facing death had made me more determined to live life, acknowl-
edging my blessings. She had been forced to give up everything—
her husband, her children, her family and friends, and her
teaching, which she dearly loved. Still, she seemed to conquer
the fear of death and gave all of us some of her strength. My sister, Rachel, and I marveled at Jan's bravery and optimism, even
to the end.

One day, Jan's husband showed us her favorite Psalm in
the Bible. She loved the entire Psalm, but he said Psalm 30:5 was
the verse she especially claimed for her own. After her death,
Rachel and I decided to have part of the verse inscribed on Jan's
monument: " . . . weeping may endure for a night, but joy cometh
in the morning." To all of us this partial verse described our
sister's faith. I did not know then how much my own faith
would be tested nor what this verse would come to mean to me.

CHAPTER 17
THE MEDICATION

Of all the parts of my life with Weston, this is the most difficult to relate and came nearest to being dismissed as necessary to the book. The difficulty in writing this part is probably due to the ambivalent feelings I have about finding out what might have gone terribly awry with my child because of the medication he was taking and my feelings of guilt for the role I played in his taking it. Drugs for treatment of illness are so complicated to us that we as patients and parents of children being treated find it simpler to trust our physicians implicitly in administering them by proxy.

I find it amazing that parents such as I, because of our ignorance, allow our children to be medicated for long periods of time with no counseling, no therapy, no real diagnosis of the problem. Learning disabled children are still being grouped together, no matter the discrepancy in severity of different children's problems, and it seems that most are prescribed the same medicine with an "It's done. Let's see what happens" attitude.

In the case of my child, I cannot honestly write about his life and death if I do not elaborate about the years of medication and the possibility that his suicide may be directly linked to the effects of the medication.

When a person is given a prescription for a medication by a doctor, he takes the prescription to a pharmacist. The pharmacist fills the prescription and puts a label on the bottle which states the amount and the number of times a day the medication is to be taken. Then, unless the doctor or pharmacist gives a few words of his own, the label is all the information a person has about the drug he is taking. The warnings and adverse effects that could result from taking the drug in combination with other drugs or could result from pre-existing conditions in the patient, etc., are only on the physician inserts (from the pharmaceutical companies) which are given to physicians and pharmacists. Seldom, if ever, does a doctor or pharmacist give a patient (or caregiver of the patient) a copy of the insert distributed by the manufacturer of the drug. How can a person possibly know about the side effects that could result from taking a specific medication? **Only after Wes' death did I go to a pharmacist and secure a copy of the insert for physicians about Imipramine and Ritalin and read about the warnings and possible side effects and other vital information that I needed to have known.**

I can only describe the emotions of relief and hope I felt upon leaving the doctor's office with that first prescription four years previously. The kind doctor had taken a great deal of time with both Weston and me, talking, listening, testing, explaining, even going into case histories and his own personal experience. I sensed he had told these things and seen the same problems many times before. I watched him closely as he spoke and realized that he knew at once the depth of Weston's problems and feared a resistance from me to the treatment he intended to prescribe. But resistance was the farthest thing from my mind. No one knew better than I that Weston was not progressing normally. The natural fear of medication, particularly an innate substance which was meant to affect the brain of my child, did not pose near the dread as did the possible unalterability of his condition. I mainly feared the possibility that his problems were my fault.

One might call it blind faith in the turn of events that here, at last, was our release, mine and Weston's, from frustration, from forgetting and reminding, from the nightly bedwetting and the daily sheet washing, the facial tics, and the throat noises. Maybe the medication would be our salvation.

And so, I filled the prescription for a low dosage of Imipramine Hydrochloride and gave Weston his first pill before bedtime. I sent the envelope containing the teacher's checklist and the note to his fifth grade teacher as the doctor instructed me to.

Wes would be monitored at school and at home, and we were both to report back to the doctor any results in two weeks.

We were pioneers. Wes was a test subject. To reap the benefits we must experience the fear of the unknown. This, in a nutshell, was what was really happening.

The results were no less than dramatic at home. Within just three to four days the facial tics were disappearing, and the bedwetting stopped. Weston's teacher reported that she had already noted improvement in his attention span, his handwriting, and his interaction with his classmates. At home I watched for signs that he himself noticed or was aware of any personal changes from the "memory pill." I saw no evidence nor heard any comments from him, but I was elated at what I observed. Wes was less anxious because he experienced fewer mistakes, fewer criticisms and stares, fewer exasperated reactions to his mere presence. I was less anxious, too.

Wes, at ten years, never questioned the fact that the little pills were handed to him each night or each morning to "cure" the unknown malady from which he suffered. We never discussed together his self-conscious feelings about the cessation of the bedwetting or anything connected to the medicine. Although he was really not that young in years, he simply did not question or complain about the medicine.

Drugs, as I have said, are very difficult to write about. There are warnings, indications, contraindications, precautions, usage in children, usage in pregnancy and a whole list of possible adverse reactions, psychiatric and allergic, and even seizures. Before taking any drug, overdosage must be considered, symptoms and treatment, with which practically none of us concern ourselves. In the case of most medications prescribed for the learning disabled child, the clinical pharmacology states that "the mechanism of action is not definitely known," or in the doctor's words, "We don't know how it works with these children, but it does."

The clinical pharmacology of Imipramine Hydrochloride describes the drug as one that "does not appear to act primarily by stimulation of the central nervous system." Although the way in which it reacts with the nervous system is not understood, the clinical effect is thought to be due to "potentiation of adrenergic synapses by blocking uptake of norepinephrine at nerve endings." The mode of action of the drug in controlling childhood enuresis [bedwetting] is thought to be apart from its anti-depressant effect.

Of course, it did not occur to me that my child might be or was depressed—saddened and discouraged by failures or being taunted and laughed at by other children, yes, but not actually depressed. However, the indications of the drug prescribed by the doctor were for the relief of symptoms of depression. "Endogenous depression (developing within the cell wall, or relating to metabolism)," the **physician's insert** reads, "is more likely to be alleviated than other depressive states." Wes had become happier, more relaxed, but I did not altogether know whether the drug altered his emotions as well.

What about side effects? Warnings were on the physician's insert, **which I had not seen**, but in the beginning my discussion with the doctor only alerted me to the fact that over-medication might result in drowsiness. All parents are aware that in most drugs a maximum dose should not be exceeded in childhood, or there may be mild or even dire consequences. I trusted that the doctor was careful not to prescribe too much of this medicine, so I did not concern myself with knowing anymore about it. **As I have stated, I did not actually study (nor was I privy to) the physician's prescription insert until after Weston's death.** Relating symptoms and side effects to the doctor by telephone was my only input when, in fact, I needed to know **thoroughly beforehand** what to be concerned with in the medication of my son and to be aware of the possibility of future problems.

Typical communications were:

Me: Doctor, the facial tics, throat noises, and teeth grinding have returned. (These are symptoms of a disorder now known as Tourette Syndrome.)

Doctor: Let's increase the medicine to ___ mg/day, and call
          me in two weeks.

                    * * * * * * * *

Me: Doctor, Wes is falling asleep on his desk at school.
          He's hard to wake up in the morning, too.

Doctor: Let's decrease the medicine to ___ mg and try
          giving it to him at night one hour before bedtime.

                    * * * * * * * *

Me: Doctor, Wes does well in the morning at school,
          but the teacher says he doesn't do well in the
          afternoon.

Doctor: Let's divide the dosage into ___ mg in the
          morning and ___ mg about noon or before lunch.

Sending medication to school was a practice I never liked,
even when the children were recovering from illness that required completion of a prescription after they were well enough
to go back to school. I remembered my own experiences with
medicated children when I taught school were oftentimes unpleasant and embarrassing for the child. I did not want Wes
exposed to such experiences after he had begun to do so well.

I soon stopped sending Wes to school with a pill. It was
becoming quite evident, anyway, as the school term ended that
the effectiveness of the medication might be decreasing with
continued administration. I worried that all the good it did would
fade away in a short while.

The teacher was asked to write an evaluation of the
change she observed in Weston, and I was overjoyed with her
letter [see page 35]. I quickly copied the letter and forwarded it
to the doctor who, I knew, would feel as much satisfaction as he
had anticipated from his diagnosis and treatment of Wes. It

had been a struggle for us all, but it was working.

The first frightening experience with Weston's reaction to
the drug came that summer before his sixth grade year. As
usual, the children spent a lot of time in the sun (which, in the
physician's insert, is not recommended for patients taking Imipramine). Wes called me back to his bedroom one night. He said
his heart was "pounding in his ears." He couldn't go to sleep. He
was not in any pain, had no fever, and was not sweating. I put
my ear to his chest and thought I detected a racing beat of the
heart. The next morning I did not give Weston his medicine, even
though there was no way for me to know that this heart complaint was a side effect of the Imipramine. I called the doctor and
told him what was happening. I reminded him, too, that Wes'
pediatric heart specialist (in Baton Rouge) had discovered a
murmur in Weston's heart when he was just a toddler. (Only a
few months before Wes' death, our family doctor examined Wes
for another sore throat and expressed concern that the murmur
was still pronounced and wanted me to consult a specialist.)
Interestingly, the Imipramine prescription insert reads, "Extreme caution should be used when the drug is given to: patients
with cardiovascular disease because of the possibility of conduc-
tion defects, arrhythmias (an alteration in rhythm of the heartbeat either in time or force), myocardial infarction, strokes and
tachycardia (a relatively rapid heart action). These patients," it
warns, "require cardiac surveillance at all dosage levels of the
drug."

When I called Wes' doctor, he immediately agreed with me
that it could possibly be the Imipramine that was causing the
racing heartbeat, but just to be on the safe side, he would call in
a change of medication to Endep. I was to call him about the
results. From that time forward, probably due to my alarm and
the doctor's cautionary treatment, there was a change from
Endep to Tofranil (a generic form of Imipramine), trials with
Cylert, and finally Ritalin. We always returned to Imipramine
when Weston could tolerate it. **For the first time, I felt a
danger was posed to my child from the intake of these
drugs.** The danger was minimized by the confidence exuded by

the doctor, but annoying fear on my part was still there. (I learned after Wes died that the doctor felt more comfortable with
Imipramine because of the benefits of its anti-depressant effect.)

I bought a divided pill dispenser to aid us both, as well as
babysitters, and Daddy and grandparents when he visited them.
I filled the dispenser for Monday through Sunday. Each slot
contained his "memory pill," vitamin, and when ill, Tylenol, an
antibiotic or other prescription. Wes was prone to injuries, so
there was an abundance to add. This reminded me of watching
my grandmother while she lived in a nursing home simply dump
a small paper cup of pills into her mouth everyday and swallow
them unquestioningly, believing them necessary and good for
her.

Wes became adept at swallowing many pills together, too.
At breakfast each morning, the pill dispenser was shoved toward
him, or the pills were placed alongside his plate. He did not
balk often but accepted this as a routine inconvenience, sometimes only complaining, "Aw, Mom, so many?"

As a fourteen year old, however, the taking of his pills
was different. He sat next to his sister at the kitchen bar and
visited with cousins or friends, spending the weekend, who
watched him take these pills and wondered what was wrong
with him. I suppose he wondered, too. I know he felt odd and
awkward. I was the culprit (as I thought of myself after he died)
who prepared the setting for a teenager to become insecure and
self-destructive, and if that were not bad enough, I gave him
the medication meant to help him but which may have destroyed him.

Imipramine "may enhance the CNS depressant effects of
alcohol. Therefore, it should be borne in mind that the dangers
inherent in a suicide attempt or accidental overdosage with the
drug may be **increased** for the patient who uses excessive
amounts of alcohol," the physician's insert states. Even though
it is widely known in all sectors of our society that teenagers
are susceptible to the social use of alcohol, the doctor did not
choose to broach the subject as yet, nor discuss the dread possibility of teen suicide attempts. **I believe it is vitally important**

**that parents of adolescents taking Imipramine be warn-
ed of suicidal impulses.** The omission of this vital detail
about alcohol in my consultations with the doctor prior to Weston's death bothered me so much immediately after Wes died
that I went to see him just one week after burying my child to ask
why I had not been forewarned or alerted to the possibility of
such adverse effects from the drug. The doctor told me that we
have only begun to scrape the surface of the nature of chemical
imbalance and how to treat the resulting brain dysfunction. He
said that when he describes these children as "disturbed," he
only means they are bothered by whatever is going on in their
minds, not that they are psychotic. **He also said that Wes could
not have been treated with counseling because his problem was not psychological** and that Weston's suicide was **not**
a result of his environment or something we did or didn't do. The
doctor stated that when Wes died, we still did not know the
appropriate amounts of the drug he needed or the one best suit-
ed for him.

   "It should be kept in mind that the possibility of suicide in
seriously depressed patients is inherent in the illness and may
persist until significant remission occurs. Such patients should
be carefully supervised during the early phase of treatment
with Imipramine Hydrochloride, and may require hospitaliza-
tion," the physician's insert also states. This tiny paper insert
in the tiniest print (almost impossible to read) also warns of
reported adverse reactions, such as anxiety, emotional instabil-
ity, restlessness, agitation, manic episodes, and possibility of
suicide (as already mentioned). It also warns that prescriptions
for Imipramine should be written for the smallest amount fea-
sible and in adolescents, generally no more than 100 mg/day.
Weston, at the time of his death, was taking 100 mg/day.

   There were other side effects that manifested themselves in
Wes and should be mentioned, also. He developed frequent sore
throats and high fever, at which times I wanted to discontinue the
Imipramine until he got well. The additional medicine prescribed
by family physicians gave him the feeling of being dragged down
by so many pills.

In the case of Ritalin, safety in children, especially very young children, has not been established; yet, for approximately the past ten years, it has been commonly prescribed with few restraints for the so-called hyperactive child. Even though the physician's insert clearly states that "Ritalin should be periodically discontinued to assess the child's condition" and "treatment should not and need not be indefinite and usually may be discontinued after puberty," parents still report that teachers and school nurses insist that the child have a daily dose in some cases, or they may not remain in the classroom.

Ritalin is a mild central nervous system stimulant. It presumably activates the brain stem arousal system and cortex to produce its stimulant effect. For Attention Deficit Disorders (previously known as Minimal Brain Dysfunction, MBD, in children), Ritalin is indicated as an integral part of a total treatment program which typically includes other remedial measures—psychological, educational, social—for a stabilizing effect in children with a behavioral syndrome characterized by the following group of developmentally inappropriate symptoms: moderate to severe distractibility, short attention span, hyperactivity, emotional lability, and impulsivity. Learning may or may not be impaired, but in the involvement of a chronic history of these symptoms over a period of time, drug treatment is indicated for more and more children in our schools today. The CIBA Pharmaceutical Company's physician insert for Ritalin states: "Certainly diagnosis must be based upon a complete history and evaluation of the child and not solely on the presence of one or more of these characteristics." Drug treatment is not indicated for all children with this syndrome. Common sense would dictate that many of these "symptoms" are natural responses to the child's home life or circumstances. Stimulants are not intended for use in the child who exhibits symptoms secondary to environmental factors and/or primary psychiatric disorders, including psychosis. "Appropriate educational placement is essential and psychological intervention is generally necessary. When remedial measures alone are insufficient, the decision to prescribe stimulant medication depends upon the physician's assessment of the chronicity and severity of the child's symptoms." But today, even a surface investigation of our schools, both rural and urban, reveals the more prevalent use of Ritalin to treat the learning disabled, calm the hyperkinetic child, or alleviate symptoms of Minimal Brain Dysfunction (Attention Deficit Disorder).

Under WARNINGS, the insert continues: "Sufficient data on safety and efficacy of long-term use of Ritalin in children are not yet available. Although a casual relationship has not been established, suppression of growth (ie, weight gain, and/or height) has been reported with the long-term use of stimulants in children. Therefore, patients requiring long term therapy should be carefully monitored. . . . Ritalin should not be used in children under 6 years of age."

More importantly, and the words jumped off the page at me (as minute as they were), "Ritalin should not be used for severe depression of either exogenous [external] or **endogenous** [internal] origin. Clinical experience suggests that in psychotic children, administration of Ritalin may exacerbate symptoms of behavior disturbance and thought disorder. . . . Human pharmacologic studies have shown that Ritalin may inhibit the metabolism of . . . antidepressants (**imipramine**, desipramine). **Downward dosage adjustments of these drugs may be required when given concomitantly with Ritalin.**"

There were days at the end of Weston's life when we jumped from Imipramine to Ritalin and back to Imipramine again (after checking with the doctor) because in my "observations" I saw Wes as being overstimulated. One night soon after he had been taking Ritalin, he ran back and forth between his bedroom and the washroom, washing and drying his new clothes. Shea and I looked at each other because we had never seen him do anything like that before. He became highly excitable and began to show uncharacteristic mood swings, slamming doors and violently reacting to aggravations. Even a simple computer game would cause him to scream and groan loudly, nearly moved to tears because he could not master it. I called the doctor. I couldn't stand the results I saw from the Ritalin although his marks in school had been excellent. I breathed a sigh of relief when he told me to fill a prescription for 100 mg/day for Tofranil (a generic form of Imipramine). Less than two weeks later, Wes was dead.

I equate my feelings about the loss of my son after all of the trial and error medicating that took place for nearly four and one-half years with one who has lost a child to cancer or heart disease after all of the tests, surgery, chemotherapy, and prayers failed to save him. Like the parents of terminally ill children, I feel regret and anger. Should we have allowed them to go through so much? Should we have followed the doctor's advice in all areas? Was it worth it? Could I have done something else and spared my child the discomfort, fear, and even his life?

I know that regret and anger are wasted emotions. To place blame is futile, and to blame oneself when there is so much grief to deal with is the most destructive thing of all. I have learned to accept my ignorance and helplessness, to live with the experience that I had to face and move on. Months and months of clinical depression engulfed me, but I did not take any medicine. I allowed myself to suffer enormously. Yet, when I think how close I myself came to suicide, I know this was probably folly not to seek help and not to have a medication that could help me. Medicine has a valuable place in our society. In treatment of depression, schizophrenia, and yes, the learning disabled children in our schools, the medical profession has made great strides and spared much misery. It is not the medication that I question. It is the **ignorance of what harm it does and can do** that continues to haunt me because of the way my child died. An adolescent child on medication, without question, should be counseled; his parents should be cautioned to watch for the signs of depression. When appropriate, a time for weaning the child from medication should be planned and discussed. It is hard for me to forget that none of these actions was taken.

The early 20th century physician Sir William Osler said, "Man is the pill-taking animal." We exist in a world now that gives nodding approval to the dispensation of pills, tablets, and capsules for every complaint from allergy to sleeplessness.

Georgetown University's Dr. Brian Doyle notes in a recent

newspaper article: "When you combine the wish for medicine and instant relief with physicians who want to help people with anxiety, bingo!" He further states that anxiety is the most common symptom of psychological distress. I think children, like adults, have anxiety attacks. They worry and fear that they somehow don't measure up in school, with friends, with parents, with God. This distress, coupled with real problems that indicate the child really doesn't measure up, can be catastrophic. Parents, teachers, ministers, etc., must be made aware of and taught how to recognize the symptoms of depression in teenagers when the teenagers feel they can't cope with the pressures surrounding them.

In John Q. Baucom's book, *Fatal Choice*, he discusses adolescent stress and challenges, the "self-esteem connection," but he repeatedly goes back to depression. He says that when a teenager begins to act out depression, he gives his parents signs that are meant to say, "Hey, I'm in trouble. Deep trouble." He also states: "In later adolescence, depression comes to take on more classical symptoms, but is still difficult to detect. The teenager may describe a sense of overwhelming boredom, lack of concentration, lack of energy, or a general report of lethargy and isolation." In the last few weeks of Weston's life, he would come home and sleep after school; his grades fell steadily; he did not want to do anything, sometimes even refusing to come to the telephone to talk to his friends; and, he drank when not supervised. Although Baucom goes on to say, "Some of those symptoms are admittedly expressed by all teens, . . . if we observe them in combination with other symptoms . . . we certainly need to take notice." Had I known what I needed to know about Weston, as well as been informed or perceptive enough to observe adolescent depression, could I have saved my son? Baucom admits in the appendix of his book: "Generally it is easier to notice depression as people grow older. Adolescents will more readily attempt to mask or disguise despair."

Weston's psychological distress was secondary to my own at that time, I admit. A single mother trying to rear two teenagers, both rather unpredictable, a job filled with pressures to meet sales quotas and fill the role of manager both in an office and in the field, a senior graduating from high school with all the festivities and stress that surround such an event, not to mention feeble attempts at a social life of my own—all of these made me an unlikely candidate as a mother who would recognize much of anything more than hunger. But looking back, I guess I did the best I could. I still wonder.

As with most parents, Wes' education was foremost in my mind. After all, school is the major part of children's lives. I suppose I proved that years ago when I refused to allow him to be held back from first grade. So, when I heard him saying, "I don't want to take the pills anymore," I translated this rebellion to mean, "I don't care if I make F's and D's," not "I'm unhappy with myself." I wanted to counsel him, to ask him questions, but his angry response and leave-me-alone-about-it attitude hindered me from going ahead.

The truth is that the only thing I knew for sure about the "memory pill" in the adolescent years of Weston's life is that the pills had value in alleviating educational difficulties and in appropriate classroom behavior. When I remember Wes' own words, "You don't even know what it [the medication] does," it seems so prophetic that I will never, never know if the doctor and I missed something desperately important.

CHAPTER 18

May 2, 1989
(Two years after my son's suicide)

It is hard to believe that so soon I have observed the second anniversary of my son's death. The tragedy still haunts me, but I reflect upon his life with more frequency now. This month I discovered the song, *"Vincent," and found Weston's own journey related in the words.

The song is sung by Don McLean to a haunting melody which pierced my heart. It tells the story of how the artist, Vincent Van Gogh, struggled with life and tried to bring his interpretation of its beauty and its agony alive in his work. He expressed himself only on the canvas. Then he destroyed himself by suicide.

The song begins:

"Starry, starry night . . ."

It was a starry night that May 2 when Wes died. A full moon. Each full moon brings back his strange and sudden death—a reminder that he was a "moon child," born in July and how he loved the night. Wes also loved the stars, and he wrote a poem when he was only eight years old about the mystery that a single star held for him. He would sit in the yard for hours, watching the silent stars through the telescope that his

Used with permission of Music Corporation of America.

Grandmother Sandefer gave him one Christmas. What were his thoughts? Did he yearn for the faraway peaceful heavens that the stars floated through?

The song continues:

> "Paint your palette blue and gray.
> Look out on a summer's day
> With eyes that know
> The darkness in my soul.
>
> Shadows on the hills
> Sketch the trees and daffodils,
> Catch the breeze and the winter chills
> In colors on the snowy living land. . . ."

The song reminds me that Weston once wanted to paint. He was thirteen. I still have the easels, brushes, paint, and unused canvases I bought, hoping that his interest would not wane. I can still recall his sitting intently in the brightly lit game room with the small picture in front of him on which he was working. His big feet with "sneakers" were awkwardly turned in as he bent over the artist's easel with no small effort to produce a work of art. This memory brings me happiness although no artistic creations from that short period exist. He destroyed them all.

I listen to the song's soft refrain:

> "Now, I understand what you
> Tried to say to me,
> How you suffered for your sanity,
> How you tried to set them free. . . ."

Why did these words capture my imagination and make me weep for Weston? Because he did suffer; he did try to tell me. His death freed me in a way. The anxiety for him was extinguished.

"They would not listen;
They did not know how.
Perhaps they'll listen now. . . ."

A burden, recurring at the end of each stanza . . . How Wes struggled to find his place, to break out of his living hell! He even tried to relate to others at the last the hardships he was having to endure as depression darkened his young life.

"Now, I understand
What you tried to say to me,
How you suffered for your sanity,
How you tried to set them free.

They would not listen;
They did not know how.
Perhaps, they'll listen now. . . ."

Wes attempted to tell his friends, his sister, all of us, in muted ways, how miserable and unhappy he was.

"Mom, you never listen to me! Why doesn't anyone ever ask me how I feel?" I heard his words. I did listen. I did not know it mattered so much.

"For they could not love you,
But still your love was true.
And when no hope was left in sight
On that starry, starry night,
You took your life . . ."

My son took his life. It was sad and needless and left us wondering if, at almost fifteen years of age, he even knew why or what he was doing.

"But I could've told you, Vincent,
This world was never meant
For one as beautiful as you. . . ."

If I could only tell Wes how much I loved him, how beautiful he was. Did he not know? I did tell him, but children, too, have a way of not hearing.

"They would not listen;
They're not listening still.
Perhaps, they never will. . . ."

CHAPTER 19

"Mom, are you all right?" My daughter's anxious expression was such that I answered "yes" and held her close to reassure her. It was the first night after Weston's death—the first night of many that I wondered, "Will I be all right? Will I make it?"

In our family to be "all right" is an expression frequently used. We don't say "I'm okay" to each other, for to be okay is just "okay." But to be "all right" is overall better and denotes present and future all at once. The last question I asked my son was, "Will you be all right?" I sensed his need as only a mother can, I suppose, but at the same time I missed the urgency completely.

In the aftermath, I can only accept the fact that Wes wasn't "all right," and I will never be able to do a thing about it. I know well the goblins who pointed the finger of blame that Iris Bolton wrote about in her book, *My Son, My Son*. I know so well how long it takes to forgive oneself. I presumed my guilt because there was really no one to let me know I was blameless.

Now, over two years later, I look back on the changes that my fourteen-year-old son's death wrought in my life and marvel that I am "all right." After traveling up the rungs of the grief ladder, slipping and falling back down, then trying again, I see the recovery I have struggled for is attainable.

I have written pages and pages on the subject of my son's death and how it affected me. I do not know exactly how his death touched the lives of others. I do know that his sister, Shea, then only seventeen, the one person perhaps closest to him in this world, was deeply hurt and bewildered by the suicide. Her young life was unfairly altered by so much tragedy early on. As shattered as she was, Shea was the one most understanding of Weston's need to leave this life. She was strong and held her grief intact, outwardly. Once she told me that she grieved all the time. I was so comforted by her calm discussions with me concerning his death. I took it for granted that she fared better than I. Later, I was to realize that, like her mother, she held it in, wrote about her loss and feelings of guilt, but showed a natural face to her mother, friends, and family.

Mourning for my dead child encompassed every facet of my life. From mealtime to bedtime, schooltime to churchtime, fresh onslaughts of grief waves were generated. Writing this has made me cry aloud and wipe away tears again. I think of the fourteen years of his life and my life, locked away in my heart. Remnants of it are packed away in a storage room behind the house—red-white-and-blue bookends, red furniture I painted that was once his father's, the American soldiers, John Wayne dolls and pictures, his grandfather's sword and bugle, his bottle collection, his rock collection— things I can't bear to part with or look at.

After I took stock of the life offered him, I realized that the material things did not matter at all. The lifeless body I found clad in shorts and T-shirt, lying in the middle of his all-American boy's room, made a silent protest against this ordinary middle-class environment. His room was filled with computer equipment, rock tapes, the latest in high top tennis shoes and clothes, books, collections, a bulletin board covered with Florida vacation pictures and Happy Birthday cards, all spattered with blood.

Suicide says to the survivors: "I do not care about material things anymore and maybe never did. My life was not made happy by the things you could buy or sacrifice time for. My life was not made happy by your love and concern. My life in this home was not happy. You and your useless offerings cannot keep me here!" All that remains is an unspoken goodbye.

One might question, "Well, if you are getting better, why do you try to write about his death?" I now know how something alien and horrible feels. Now I empathize and sympathize differently. I look at any pathos from a different viewpoint, but after Wes' death, I wondered why I never related at all to the pain that bereft parents feel, why I never knew the duration or intensity of such grief, and why I never took the suicidal teenager's story to heart or examined it in my mind. To me those were tragedies that may or may not have had reason, but my family was not touched by it. Until now.

Curiously, I want other parents to know that in their lonely grief someone truly understands. I hear of recent teenage suicides since Weston's death by way of the news media or word of mouth, and I want to contact the mothers, especially, and say to them, "This is the way it is. Don't torture yourself. You'll live with pain now, but it will get better. You must hold on." I want to share with them and say "Try these things" or "Read these books."

Usually, the survivor of suicide thinks his individual experience must be worse than all others. The knowledge that suicide experiences have happened to other fellow humans doesn't help. The survivor perceives his situation to be different and more tragic than others or that other survivors are just able to deal with it better than they. This is a special curse that suicide delivers and the reason many survivors band together in small groups. For others, they believe, the circumstances must be easier to bear: They had spouses to lean on; there was another son or daughter to give comfort; another child was born later; there were material possessions to compensate; they had the ability to get away from a stressful job, to travel; they had religious strength to draw from; and on and on.

Then they visit a coping group and find that they were wrong; hardly anyone handles a suicide well, despite his/her circumstances. After discovering this, the survivor can let the barriers down. Feeling that it must be easier for others to cope with my son's death than it was for me prevented me from opening up to family, counselors, or friends about the raw reality of it and what it was doing to me. I wasn't "handling" it, and this was a source of fear and embarrassment—all the more reason to keep it hidden. It wasn't until much later that I read about the "crazies" grief can cause. I thought I was weak and regressing each time it happened to me.

I have been there. I have told my story, but now we must concentrate on you. You must work through what has happened and find your own peace. Beginning now, allow yourself time to be near your loved one as you knew him or her before. You, and only you, can know how compelled you are to be able to dwell on this person. Whether husband, wife, child, sister, brother, grandparent, grandchild, or best friend, your relationship with that loved one was, and is, a vital part of your life. It cannot be denied now that this person is gone. You must allow yourself to think about it. You may think that as close as you were, as strong as your love was, as much as you trusted and cared, you did not matter to them. **You did matter**. You were there for your loved one in the ways that you learned from life's experiences as they were offered to you. Nothing could prepare you for suicide.

Did you try to talk, to understand, to show you cared, while at the same time trying to live your own life as best you could? These thoughts are normal. Very few people have any measure of professional astuteness. The ability to detect severe depression or the roots of problems with which adolescents and adults suffer is rare in humans. The sufferer hides these feelings, purposely, and many times does not understand them himself. Negative feelings are difficult to share, especially with loved ones who will worry. Life is not perfect. People are not perfect. People fail, even with the best of intentions.

You may be saying to yourself over and over again that somehow you failed. This cannot be altogether true. Your loved one did not allow you to succeed. You were unknowingly fighting a battle with a death wish, a seed that only he or she planted and nurtured with all of the negative aspects of his environment that he could gather, shunning the hope, the encouragement, the advice or discipline you and any others may have offered. Possibly the death wish grew stronger beneath a disguise that told you everything was proceeding naturally, although with complications. Only he or she really knew how unnaturally the fledgling plant was thriving within. Roots of bitterness, fear, self-doubt, low self-esteem, and unworthiness crowded out the weakening little plants of hope and anticipation of a brighter day.

The plant had become a shadowing overgrowth, letting no life, love, or happy memories penetrate. Existence like this is extremely painful. The pain must be controlled, or it must be killed. The suicide victim killed the strangling plant and in so doing sacrificed his life. Whether he meant to or not, he also sacrificed a part of yours. Can that now be helped?

I read many books and articles in my search to ease my own heartache. The following are some that I found to be extremely helpful: *My Son, My Son* by Iris Bolton; *Hope for Bereaved* handbook, 1342 Lancaster Avenue, Syracuse, New York 13210; *Fatal Choice* by John Q. Baucom; *Getting Through the Night* by Eugenia Price; *When Bad Things Happen to Good People* by Harold S. Kushner; *To Help You Through the Hurting* by Marjorie Holmes; "A Gift of Hope" by Robert L. Veninga; and, *After Suicide* by John H. Hewitt, which, in my opinion, is a manual about surviving suicide to be read and reread.

A loved one's suicide utterly tears away the security of the survivor's life. We need to have courage, peace, strength, and be loved to again face life. You will once more receive all of these, even though you may feel you can't trust life now. Concentrate on what was good and positive in your loved one's life. In the case of my son, it was a very short life, just over fourteen years. I listed on paper the things I knew he loved, valued, and enjoyed. This was an exorcism of sorts because I had to force myself to remember the good things for a long while and crowd out the fresh new memory of a tragic death brought about by a multitude of unfortunate circumstances.

I suggest that you write down a list of things your loved one liked to do, to eat, or to watch on TV. List gifts he cherished, books he liked to read, favorite vacation spots, types of cars he liked, special friends, etc. Make your list as long as you possibly can. Keep the list and add to it as you remember. You will see many experiences you shared go down on paper. These things will also point out to you, privately, that life was ordinary, no matter how extraordinary the death. Happy memories will help push out the painful thoughts.

The things you could or should have done will always be

missing from this list. You could not see into the future. Under the best of circumstances you cannot be all things to anyone. A hard lesson to learn and accept when dealing with another person's life once so intertwined with yours is: You don't get any second chances. Your loved one shut you out. He chose death, but he wasn't capable, at that last moment, of thinking about anyone or anything except that he and everybody else would be better off without him.

There are many causes of suicide, and yet, surprisingly, there are suicides seemingly without any cause that can be pinpointed, except for what must have been in that person's mind. You will want to understand it, to accept it, but you really can't. Your family and friends are horrified by it and so, they too, will make efforts to help you accept it. They will say things that are meant to help but will, in fact, hurt deeply because none of it makes sense. Of course, life can become so intolerable that a human being eventually rejects another day of it. However, just look around at the abject people who live in squalor, depressed surroundings, and abusive environments with overwhelming problems; they choose to live. That is right. The choice **for** life must be made. No matter how much influence you had, no matter the part you played, you never wanted or expected your loved one to choose death.

Now we come to the moment of truth. You will want more than anything else just to talk to your loved one and tell him how you feel about things. Problems were left unsolved, plans were left unfinished, and you are left with questions that only he or she can answer for you. Last, you did not get to say "goodbye." Perhaps there was a note left for you. If so, or if not, you can write a response. This is your right. Write a note or letter in answer. Write it and be done with it.

You must be careful not to obsessively dwell on the death itself. Suicide is violence, and violence shatters reason. The suicide must be faced with the realization that this happened to someone very important to you by **his own choice and not yours**, even though you are the one who is left to live with it.

In understanding and accepting the suicidal death of a loved one, you may be absolved of responsibility, but it does not make missing him less difficult to bear. Although I have lived through some sad times, I try hard to remember the good so that I will have the strength and courage, *with God's help*, to continue to live and to grow. Through the living and growing, I pray that the seeds may be sown to make new memories to cherish and share with those I love.

Psalm 121:1-2 says, "I will lift up mine eyes unto the hills, from whence cometh my help. My help cometh from the Lord, which made heaven and earth." I have often wondered why the psalmist looked to the hills. Now I know it is because he was in a valley, and God was there. Without the valleys there would be no hills. Without the tears and pain, no laughter, joy, or pleasures ever realized would be as sweet. Neither would there be the desire for survival and preservation as described in this psalm.

My five-year-old Weston cried out, "Mama, I want my soul to keep," and so it shall, for verses 5 and 7 of Psalm 121 assure us "The Lord is thy keeper . . . he shall preserve thy soul."

I have survived. You will survive. I am "all right." You will be "all right."

—END—

TEARS ARE THE PROOF OF LIFE

"How long will the pain last?" a brokenhearted mourner asked me.

"All the rest of your life," I had to answer truthfully.

We never quite forget . . . No matter how many years pass, we remember. The loss of a loved one is like a major operation; part of us is removed and we have a scar for the rest of our lives.

This does not mean that the pain continues at the same intensity. There is a short while, at first, when we hardly believe it; it is rather like when we cut our hand. We see the blood flowing, but the pain has not set in yet. So when we are bereaved, there is a short while before the pain hits us. But when it does, it is massive in its effect. Grief is shattering.

Then the wound begins to heal. It is like going through a dark tunnel. Occasionally, we glimpse a bit of light up ahead, then lose sight of it awhile, then see it again, and one day we merge into the light. We are able to laugh, to care, to live. The wound is healed, so to speak, the stitches are taken out, and we are whole again.

But not quite. The scar is still there and the scar tissue, too.

As the years go by, we manage. There are things to do, people to care for, tasks that call for our full attention. But the pain is still there, not far below the surface. We see a face that looks familiar, hear a voice that has echoes, see a photograph in an album, see a landscape that once we saw together, visit places we once visited, and it is though the knife were in the wound again.

But not so painfully. And mixed with joy, too. Because remembering a happy time is not all sorrow; it brings back happiness with it.

How long will it last?

All the rest of your life. But the thing to remember is that not only the pain will last, but the blessed memories as well. Tears are the proof of life. The more love, the more tears. If this be true, then how could we ever ask that the pain cease altogether? For then, the memory of love would go with it. The pain is the price we pay for love.

Author Unknown

IF YOU WOULD LIKE TO ORDER ONE OR MORE OF THESE BOOKS FOR YOURSELF OR SOMONE WHO IS GRIEVING OVER A SUICIDE, OR POSSIBLY FOR A CHURCH LIBRARY, ETC., PLEASE FILL IN THE COUPON BELOW AND SEND IT ALONG WITH A CHECK OR MONEY ORDER TO:

JACKSON ENTERPRISES
P. O. BOX 493
COUSHATTA, LOUISIANA 71019

PLEASE SEND ME _____ copies of MOM, I'M ALL RIGHT at $8.95 each plus $2.00 for handling/mailing (a total of $10.95 each). Enclosed is my check in the amount of $_____.

_____
(Name)   (Address)

_____
(City)   (State)   (Zip)

RECOMMENDED SOURCES FOR HELP OR INFORMATION:

* The Compassionate Friends
  P.O. Box 3696
  Oak Brook, Illinois   60522-3696

* American Association of Suicidology
  2459 S. Ash
  Denver, Colorado   80110

* CH.A.D.D.
  Children with Attention Deficit Disorders
  499 N.W. 70th Ave., Suite 308
  Plantation, Florida   33317

* Teen Suicide Prevention Task Force
  701 E. Main Street
  Grand Prairie, Texas   75050